BLACKOUT

'The story of a rising star's journey of self-destruction and realization, *Blackout* is gripping, alternately excruciating and funny, scary and hopeful, and beautifully written. I loved it'
Anne Lamott, author of *Small Victories*

'a dark, funny, honest-to-the-bone account of getting sober'
Buzzfeed

'Sarah Hepola's *Blackout* is the best kind of memoir: fiercely funny, full of hard-won wisdom, marked by a writer with phenomenal gifts of observation and insight. The book engages universal questions – Where do I belong? What fulfills me? – that will engage any reader'
Emily Rapp, author of *The Still Point Of The Turning World*

'Razor-sharp . . . modern, raw, and painfully real-and even hilarious . . . Hepola moves beyond the analysis of her addiction, making this the story of every woman's fight to be seen for who she really is'
Kirkus (starred review)

'One of the most anticipated pop cultural events of 2015 . . . Hepola's dark, wise and often terrifically funny insights into her own toughest experiences are unfailingly riveting, and there's no doubt in our minds that her debut memoir will be a sensation'
Salon

'One of the best books we can't wait to read in 2015'
Chicago Reader

'This is a book about welcoming yourself back from a long absence. It's a memoir, but its author is not its main character; she is a new person sprung from the ashes of another one whose alcoholic self-erasure she describes with painful honesty and charming humour. A book about freedom that will help set others free as well'
Walter Kirn, author of *Up In The Air*

'Sarah Hepola is my favorite kind of memoirist. She is a reporter with a poet's instincts, an anthropologist of her own soul. *Blackout* is a book about drinking and eventual sobriety, but it's also an exploration of the fleeting nature of the comfort we all constantly seek – comfort with the self, with others, with the whole maddening, confusing, exhilarating world. What's more, Hepola's ability to bring such precise and evocative life to the blank spaces that were her drinking blackouts is downright stunning in places. I admire this book tremendously'
Meghan Daum, author of *The Unspeakable:*
And Other Subjects Of Discussion

BLACKOUT

Remembering the Things I Drank to Forget

SARAH HEPOLA

www.tworoadsbooks.com

First published in Great Britain in 2015 by Two Roads
An imprint of John Murray Press
An Hachette UK company

2

This memoir reflects the author's life faithfully rendered to the best of her ability.
Some names and identifying details have been changed to protect the privacy of others.
The author is grateful to *Salon*, *Nerve*, and *The Morning News*, where some
of the material in *Blackout* first appeared in a different form.
*This is Water: Some Thoughts, Delivered on a Significant Occasion, about Living a
Compassionate Life* by David Foster Wallace. Copyright © 2009 by the David Foster
Wallace Literary Trust. Used by permission.

A CIP catalogue record for this title is available from the British Library

Trade Paperback ISBN 978 1 473 61608 0
Ebook ISBN 978 1 473 61609 7

Printed and bound by CPI Group (UK) Ltd, Croydon, CR0 4YY

Hodder & Stoughton policy is to use papers that are natural,
renewable and recyclable products and made from wood grown in
sustainable forests. The logging and manufacturing processes are expected
to conform to the environmental regulations of the country of origin.

Hodder & Stoughton Ltd
Carmelite House
50 Victoria Embankment
London EC4Y 0DZ

www.hodder.co.uk

FOR ANYONE WHO NEEDS IT

BLACKOUT

THE CITY OF LIGHT

I'm in Paris on a magazine assignment, which is exactly as great as it sounds. I eat dinner at a restaurant so fancy I have to keep resisting the urge to drop my fork just to see how fast someone will pick it up. I'm drinking cognac—the booze of kings and rap stars—and I love how the snifter sinks between the crooks of my fingers, amber liquid sloshing up the sides as I move it in a figure eight. Like swirling the ocean in the palm of my hand.

Somewhere near midnight, I tumble into a cab with my friend and the night starts to stutter and skip. She leans into me, the bundle of scarf around her face. It's cold, and we are squished together on the vinyl seat, too lit to care about the intimacy of our limbs. The streets are a smear through the window. The taxi meter, a red blur. How did we get back so fast? A second ago, we were laughing in the cab. And now, I'm standing on the street alone.

I walk through the front door of my hotel, into the bright squint of the lobby. My heels clickety-clak across the white stone. It's that time of night when every floor has a banana peel, and if I'm not careful, I might find my face against the ground, my hands braced beside me, and I'll have to explain to the concierge how clumsy and hilarious I am. So I walk with a vigilance I hope doesn't show.

I exchange a few pleasantries with the concierge, a bit of theater to prove I'm not too drunk, and I'm proud of how steady my voice sounds. I don't want him thinking I'm just another American girl wasted in Paris. The last thing I hear is my heels, steady as a metronome, echoing through the lobby. And then, there is nothing. Not a goddamn thing.

This happens to me sometimes. A curtain falling in the middle of the act, leaving minutes and sometimes hours in the dark. But anyone watching me wouldn't notice. They'd simply see a woman on her way to somewhere else, with no idea her memory just snapped in half.

It's possible you don't know what I'm talking about. Maybe you're a moderate drinker, who baby-sips two glasses of wine and leaves every party at a reasonable hour. Maybe you're one of those lucky fellows who can slurp your whiskey all afternoon and never disappear into the drink. But if you're like me, you know the thunderbolt of waking up to discover a blank space where pivotal scenes should be. My evenings come with trapdoors.

I don't know how much time I lose in this darkness. Or what takes place. When the curtain lifts again, this is what I see.

There is a bed, and I'm on it. The lights are low. Sheets are wrapped around my ankles, soft and cool against my skin. I'm on top of a guy I've never seen before, and we're having sex.

Hold on. Can this be right? I'm having sex with a man, and

I've never seen him before. It's like the universe dropped me into someone else's body. Into someone else's *life*. But I seem to be enjoying it. I'm making all the right sounds.

As the room comes into focus, my body completes its erotic pantomime. I collapse beside him and weave my legs through his. I wonder if I should be worried right now, but I'm not scared. I don't mean to suggest I'm brave. I mean to suggest you could break a piece of plywood over my head, and I would smile, nod, and keep going.

The guy isn't bad-looking. Slightly balding, but he has kind eyes. They glisten in the low light. And I think, whoever picked up this man, she did an OK job.

"You really know how to wear a guy out," he says. I trace a knuckle down the side of his face. It seems unfair that he should know me, and I don't know him, but I'm unsure of the etiquette. *Excuse me, but who are you, and why are we fucking?*

"I should go," I tell him.

He gives an annoyed laugh. "You just said you wanted to stay."

So I stay with the stranger in the shadows of a room I do not recognize, looking out onto a city that is not my home. The window stretches across the wall, and I stare at the twinkling lights. I smooth my hand along his chest. It seems like the polite thing to do. He strokes my hair, and brings my hand to his lips, and if anyone were watching us, we would look like two people in love.

A blackout is the untangling of a mystery. It's detective work on your own life. A blackout is: *What happened last night? Who are you, and why are we fucking?*

As I lie in the crook of his arm, I have so many questions.

But one is louder than the others. In literature, it's the question that launches grand journeys, because heroes are often dropped into deep, dark jungles and forced to machete their way out. But for the blackout drinker, it's the question that launches another shitty Saturday.

How did I get here?

WOMEN WHO DRINK

I was 33, and lying on a futon in the middle of the day watching a talk show, because I could. I was a freelance writer in New York, and I was hungover, and try to stop me.

The show was discussing roofies. GHB, Rohypnol, the date rape drugs. This was 2007, but I'd been hearing about roofies since the late '90s: odorless, colorless substances dropped into a drink to erase memory, like something out of a sci-fi movie. I'd recently seen a network crime drama in which the heroine was slipped a roofie and woke up in a dangerous man's house. Every once in a while, motherly types (including my actual mother) worried I might be vulnerable to this invisible menace. The talk show host, for one, was very concerned. *Ladies, cover your drinks.*

I had a different drinking problem, although I wouldn't have used the word "problem," at least not without air quotes. One morning, I woke up in the living room of a cute British guy's apartment. The inflatable mattress was leaking, and my ass was scraping the ground in a plastic hammock. The last thing I remembered was walking my friend Lisa to the subway the night before. She held both my hands. "Do *not* go home with that guy," she said, and I said, "I promise. Pinky swear." Then I went back into the bar, and he ordered us another round.

This was the kind of excitement I wanted from a single life in New York, the kind of excitement I was hoping to find when I left Texas at the age of 31 in a Honda loaded down with books and heartbreak. I understood the city was not the shimmering fantasia portrayed by charming Audrey Hepburn movies and Woody Allen valentines and four fancy ladies on HBO. But I wanted my own stories, and I understood drinking to be the gasoline of all adventure. The best evenings were the ones you might regret.

"I had sex with some random British dude and woke up on a leaking air mattress," I texted my friend Stephanie.

"Congratulations!" she texted back.

Awesome. High-five. Hell, yeah. These were the responses I got from female friends when I told them about my drunken escapades. Most of my friends were married by this point. Sometimes they wondered aloud what being unattached in their 30s would be like. Careening around the city at 2 am. Tilting the wide brim of a martini glass toward the sky to catch whatever plunked into it.

Being unattached in my 30s felt good. I wasn't so lonely; reality TV was quite robust that year. Design programs. Chef programs. Musicians who used to be famous dating women who hoped to become famous. That roofie talk show made it seem like being a single woman was perilous, and you had to be on guard at all times, but I was numb to terror alerts by then. Whatever horror existed in the world, I was pretty sure GHB was not my problem.

Once, I'd gotten so blasted at a party I woke up in a dog bed, in someone else's house.

"Do you think you got roofied?" my friend asked me.

"Yes," I told her. "I think someone slipped me ten drinks."

⌒⌒⌒

BOOKS ABOUT ALCOHOLISM often talk about the "hidden drinking" of women. That's been the line for decades. Bottles stashed behind the potted plant. Sips taken with shaking hands when no one is looking, because "society looks down on women who drink."

I looked up to women who drink. My heart belonged to the defiant ones, the cigarette smokers, the pants wearers, the ones who gave a stiff arm to history. In college, we drank like the boys. After college, we hung around in dive bars with our male friends, and later, when everyone grew lousy with expendable income and the freedom of having no kids, we drained bottles of cabernet over steak dinners and debated the smoothest blends of Mexican tequila.

I joined a women's book club when I was in my late 20s. It was called "Bitches and Books," which seemed funny at the time. We gathered once a month, and balanced tiny white plates of brie and crackers on our knees as we discussed Ann Patchett and Augusten Burroughs and drank wine. Rivers of wine. Waterfalls of wine. Wine and confession. Wine and sisterhood.

Wine had become our social glue, the mechanism of our bonding. We needed the wine to shut out the jackhammers of our own perfectionism and unlock the secrets we kept within. Wine was the centerpiece of dinner parties and relaxing evenings at home. It was a requirement for work events and formal festivities. Let's not even mention the word "bachelorette." Friends moved their weddings out of churches and into restaurants and bars, where waiters served champagne before the bride had even appeared. The cool mothers had chardonnay playdates and never let the demands of child rearing keep them from happy hour. DIY sites sold onesies with a wink. *Mommy drinks because I cry.*

I wrote stories about my drinking. Some were fiction, and some were painfully true, and I liked that my snappy comic tone made it hard to tell which was which. I wrote about getting wasted before 4 pm (true) and waking up after a hard-partying music festival next to Chuck Klosterman (not true), slamming shots with strangers and drinking queso from a to-go cup (more or less true). Women today are notorious for judging each other—about how we raise children, about how we look in a swimsuit, about how we discuss race, gender, or class. Yet no matter how reckless or boozing my tales were, I never felt judged for one of them. In fact, I kind of thought women looked up to me.

By the late aughts, bumbling, blotto heroines were a staple of our narratives. *Bridget Jones's Diary* was like a tree that had grown a thousand limbs. Carrie Bradshaw was a media empire. Chelsea Handler was building a savvy business brand playing the part of a woman much drunker and more foolish than she could possibly be. (Was there any book title more indicative of the moment than *Are You There Vodka? It's Me, Chelsea?* A longing for spiritual deliverance, the innocence of young adult literature, and Grey Goose.) My smart, successful female friends tore through their *Us Weeklies*, while *New Yorkers* piled on a corner table like homework, and followed the misadventures of the era's party girls. In an age of sex tapes and beaver shots, there was nothing edgy or remotely shocking about a woman like me reporting that, hey, everyone, I fell off my bar stool.

I sometimes wondered what my mother thought. "Well, I

think you exaggerate," she told me once. In the personal essay I'd just written, for example, I mentioned having six beers. "I don't think a woman can have that many drinks in one night," she said. And my mother was right—it was more like eight.

They added up fast! Two drinks at home getting ready, three drinks with dinner, three pints at the bar afterward. And those were the nights I kept count.

My mother never drank like me. She was a sipper. A one-glass-with-dinner kind of lady. She tells me she cut loose at college frat parties, dancing in her bobby socks—a phrase that suggests how wild she did *not* get—but I've never seen her drunk and couldn't imagine what it would look like. When her extended family got together, my rowdy Irish uncles gathered in a separate room, splitting a bottle of Scotch and laughing loudly enough to rattle the walls, while my mother and her sister took care of the kids. Screw that. I wanted to be the center of the party, not the person sweeping up afterward.

By the time I was old enough to drink, culture had shifted to accommodate my desires. For generations, women had been the abstainers, the watchdogs and caretakers—women were a major force behind Prohibition, after all—but as women's place in society rose, so did their consumption, and '70s feminists ushered in a new spirit of equal-opportunity drinking. Over the following decades, as men turned away from the bottle, women did not, which meant that by the twenty-first century, when it came to drinking, women had nearly closed the gender gap. A 2013 CDC report declared binge drinking a "dangerous health problem" for women 18 to 34, especially whites and Hispanics. Nearly 14 million women in the country enjoyed an average of three binges a month, six drinks at a time. That equates to a hell of a lot of book clubs.

It's worth noting that the country, as a whole, is drinking less than we used to when alcohol hit its peak in the 1970s, the result of a higher drinking age and a shift away from three-martini lunches, among other factors. But a certain group of women have made booze a very public and very integral part of their culture. Young, educated, and drunk: That was life on the ground for me.

I thought nothing of spending most evenings in a bar, because that's what my friends were doing. I thought nothing of mandating wine bottles for any difficult conversation—for any conversation at all—because that's what I saw in movies and television. Glasses of white wine had become shorthand for honest communication. *Clink, clink, here's to us.* I may have found the Hollywood empowerment tales of "you-go-girl drinking" to be patronizing, but that doesn't mean they didn't capture my value system.

Empowerment. It was an early buzzword for the twenty-first century. Everything from building schools in third-world countries to emailing pictures of your ass to strangers became empowering. For years, I kept an *Onion* story tacked above my desk: "Women Now Empowered by Everything a Woman Does." The word's ubiquity suggested how much women wanted power but how conflicted we were about getting it. Ripping your pubic hair out by the roots was empowerment. Taking Jägermeister shots at the bar was empowerment. I just wish those shots had empowered me not to trip off the curb.

I did worry I drank too much. Actually, I had worried for a long time. I slipped in a club one night and bashed my kneecap. I fell down staircases (yes, plural). Sometimes I only skidded down a few steps—*gravity problems*, I used to joke—and then a few times I sailed to the bottom like a rag doll, and I'm not sure which is crazier: that I drank as long as I did, or that I kept wearing heels.

I think I knew I was in trouble. The small, still voice inside me always knew. I didn't hide the drinking, but I hid how much it hurt.

⌒⌒⌒

I WAS 20 YEARS old when I first started worrying I drank too much. I picked up one of those pamphlets at the student health center. *Do you have a drinking problem?* I was in college. I was pretty sure everyone I knew had a drinking problem. My photo album was a flipbook of evidence: My friend Dave, with a bottle of Jim Beam to his lips. My friend Anne, passed out on the couch with a red Solo cup still upright in her hand. Heroic postures of sin and debauch.

But there was something troubling about the way I drank. Friends would inch-worm up to me on Sundays, when our apartment was still wrecked with stink and regret. *Hey. So. We need to talk.* They tried to sound casual, like we were going to chat about boys and nail polish, but the next eight words were like needles sunk into my skin. *Do you remember what you did last night?*

And so, the pamphlet. It was such a corny, flimsy thing. It had probably been languishing on that rack of good intentions since the 1980s. The language was so alarmist and paternalistic (a word I'd just learned and enjoyed using).

Have you ever had a hangover? Come on. I felt pity for the wallflower who answered no to this question. Drinking at least three times a week was as fundamental to my education as choosing a major. My friends and I didn't hang with anyone who didn't party. There was something untrustworthy about people who crossed their arms at the bacchanal.

Next question: *Do you ever drink to get drunk?* Good lord. Why else would a person drink? To cure cancer? This was stupid.

I had come to that health clinic with real fear in my heart, but already I felt foolish for being so dramatic.

Do you ever black out?

Wait, that one. That question, right there. *Do you ever black out?*

I did. I blacked out the first time I got drunk, and it happened again. And again. Some blackouts were benign, the last few hours of an evening turning into a blurry strobe. Some were extravagant. Like the one that brought me to the health clinic, after waking up in my parents' house and having no idea how I got there. Three hours, gone from my brain.

During uncomfortable conversations with my friends, I would listen in disbelief as they told stories about me that were like the work of an evil twin. *I said what? I did what?* But I didn't want to betray how little I knew. I wanted to eject from those discussions as quickly as possible, so I would nod and tell them I felt terrible about what I'd done (whatever it turned out to be). The soft language of disarmament: *I hear you. You are heard.*

Other questions in the pamphlet were sort of ridiculous. *Do you drink every day? Have you ever been sent to jail for your drinking?* This was the low stuff of gutter drunks to me. I still shopped at the Gap. I had a Winnie-the-Pooh night lamp. No, I hadn't been sent to jail, and no, I didn't drink every day, and I was relieved to find those questions there, because they felt like exemption.

I was a college kid. I loved beer, and I loved the sophisticated sting of red wine, and I loved the fine and fiery stupor of bourbon, and sometimes I got so wasted that I poured those drinks on my head while performing songs from *A Chorus Line* in some twilight state I could not recall, and in the scope of the universe and all its problems, was this really—*really*—such a big deal?

I didn't quit drinking that day. Of course I didn't. But I left the clinic with the notion that alcohol was an escalating madness, and the blackout issue was the juncture separating two kinds of drinking. One kind was a comet in your veins. The other kind left you sunken and cratered, drained of all light.

I figured if I stayed in the middle, in the gray area, I would be OK. Blacking out was bad, but it wasn't that big of a deal, right? It's not like I was the only person who ever forgot a night of drinking, right? And it's not like it happened to me *that* often.

At a party I threw a few months later, a friend danced in my living room in a giant fish costume. The next morning, as we stared at the shiny fabric in a heap on the floor, she said: Why is that costume there?

I was flooded with gratitude. *Not just me. Thank God.*

In my 20s, friends called with that hush in their voice to tell me they'd woken up beside some guy. They called after forgotten wedding receptions where the open bar had proven a little too open. *Not just me. Thank God.*

In my early 30s, I used to have brunch with a sardonic guy who actually bragged about his blackouts. He called it "time travel," which sounded so nifty, like a supernatural power. He wasn't drinking too many Long Island iced teas; he was punching a hole in the space-time continuum.

I was laughing about my blackouts by then, too. I used to joke I was creating a show called *CSI: Hangover*, because I would be forced to dig around the apartment like a crime scene investigator, rooting through receipts and other detritus to build a plausible theory of the night's events. I imagined myself crouched by the bed, wearing those blue plastic gloves and picking up each questionable item with long tweezers. *This crumpled wrapper suggests our victim was hungry*, I would say, holding the foil in the light and then giving it a long whiff. *And this has the unmistakable smell of a Beef Meximelt.*

It's weird how a woman frightened by her own blackouts becomes a woman who shrugs them off like an unpaid cable bill. But any heavy drinker understands the constant redistricting and gerrymandering of what constitutes an actual "problem." I'd come to think of blackouts as a surcharge for the grand spectacle of drinking. There was something deliciously chaotic about tossing your night up into the air and finding out the next morning what happened. Haven't you seen *The Hangover*?

But there's a certain point when you fall down the staircase, and you look around, and no one is amused anymore. By 35, I was in that precarious place where I knew I drank too much, but I believed I could manage it somehow. I was seeing a therapist, and when I talked to her about my blackouts, she gasped. I bristled at her concern. Her tone was alarmist, like the pamphlet I'd once read, but a trip to any keg party would illustrate that if blackouts doomed a person to alcoholism, then most of us were doomed.

"Everyone has blackouts," I told her.

She locked eyes with me. "No, they don't."

⌒⌒⌒

FOR MANY YEARS, I was confounded by my blackouts, but the mechanics are quite simple. The blood reaches a certain alcohol saturation point and shuts down the hippocampus. Such a peculiar word, hippocampus, like a children's book character. I imagine a beast with a twitching snout and big, flapping eyelashes. But it's actually the part of the brain responsible for making long-term memories. You drink enough, and the beast stops twitching. Shutdown. No more memories.

Your short-term memory still works, but short-term memory lasts less than two minutes, which explains why wasted people can follow a conversation from point to point, but they will repeat themselves after some time has passed, what a friend of mine calls "getting caught in the drunkard's loop." The tendency to repeat what you just said is a classic sign of a blackout, although there are others. "Your eyes go dead, like a zombie," a boyfriend once told me. "It's like you're not there at all." People in a blackout often get a vacant, glazed-over look, as though their brain is unplugged. And, well, it kind of is.

Although some people learned to detect my blackouts, most could not. Blackouts are sneaky like that. They vary from person to person, and from night to night, the same way one drunk might put a lampshade on her head while another might sit quietly and stare into the middle distance. There's no red indicator light to alert your audience when the brain is off-line.

And people in a blackout can be surprisingly functional. This is a point worth underscoring, since the most common misperception about blacking out is confusing it with passing out, losing consciousness after too much booze. But in a blackout, a person is anything but silent and immobile. You can talk and laugh and charm people at the bar with funny stories of your past. You can sing the shit out of "Little Red Corvette" on a karaoke stage. You can run your greedy hands over a man whose name you never asked. The next day, your brain will have no imprint of these activities, almost as if they didn't happen. Once memories are lost in a blackout, they can't be coaxed back. Simple logic: Information that wasn't stored cannot be retrieved.

Some blackouts are worse than others, though. The less severe and more common form is a fragmentary blackout, or "brownout," which is like a light flickering on and off in the brain. Perhaps you remember ordering your drink, but not walking to the bar. Perhaps you remember kissing that guy, but not who made the first move.

Then there are *en bloc* blackouts, in which memory is totally disabled. *En bloc* blackouts were a specialty of mine. The light goes out and does not return for hours sometimes. I usually woke up from those blackouts on the safe shores of the next morning. The only exception was the night in Paris, when I zapped back to the world in that hotel room. I didn't even know that could happen, one of the many reasons the night stayed with me so long.

We may understand the basics of a blackout, but we still don't understand the nuances and complications. Is there any territory more vast and unknowable than the human mind? Ask anyone who's lost a parent to dementia or watched a spouse suffer a brain injury. What we remember, and how and why: This is a complex puzzle best explained by people in lab coats and not a girl who used to drink so much Dos Equis she would dip raw hot dogs in guacamole and shove them in her mouth.

One of the people in lab coats is Aaron White, a leading expert on blackouts. White is the program director for college drinking research at the National Institute on Alcohol Abuse and Alcoholism, and he dispelled some of my own confusion about blackouts. I always thought my blackouts were caused by specific types of liquors. (Brown liquor, in particular.) According to White, brown liquor doesn't cause blackouts any more than clear liquor does. It's not the type of drink you put to your lips, it's the amount of alcohol in the blood and how quickly you get to that level. Fragmentary blackouts start at a blood-alcohol content around .20, while *en bloc* blackouts start around .30.

White is accustomed to people's ignorance about blackouts,

because ours is a drinking culture disconnected from the dangers of alcohol. "If they were selling some drug at the gas station that shut down areas of your brain so that you were functioning with amnesia, we wouldn't have it," White says.

Katy Perry had a hit song about a blackout in 2011. "It was a blacked-out blur," she sang, "and I'm pretty sure it ruled." But White sees blackouts another way. From a clinical perspective, he explains, a blackout is like early Alzheimer's.

The more I learned about blackouts, the more I wondered why I'd read so little about them. I've read magazine articles dissecting some drug of the moment—how ecstasy or meth or heroin hijacks the brain. I've read click-bait stories on what new drugs your teens might be using. Mothballs, bath salts. I've seen scare segments on roofies, like the one I saw on that talk show. And yet I've never read a major article or seen a television program discussing blackouts. It's a menace hiding in plain sight.

I discussed roofies with Aaron White. Roofies aren't a myth, he said, but studies suggest the fear outpaces the incidence. Turns out, "being roofied" often doesn't involve roofies at all. People just don't realize how common it is to experience a blackout. And alcohol can have troubling interactions with prescription meds. Rohypnol is in the benzodiazepine family, often prescribed for anxiety and sleep disorders. Ativan, Xanax, Lunesta—some of the most popular meds on the market—can all create an amnesiac effect when combined with booze.

My therapist was correct. Not everyone has blackouts. The majority of people will never have one in their lifetime. But blackouts are not rare in drinking circles. In fact, they're common. A 2002 study published in the *Journal of American College Health* found that among drinkers at Duke University, more than half had experienced blackouts.

I was particularly at risk, even though I didn't realize it. Blackout drinkers tend to be the ones who hold their liquor. If you bolt to the toilet after your third cosmo, or start snoring after your second margarita, you won't build up enough booze in your bloodstream to shut the machine down. I was so proud of the way I could knock 'em back. I drank fast, and I drank a lot. I was a beer-bingeing Annie Oakley slinging her empties into the trash and popping off the next bottle cap with a sly smile. *Wanna watch me go again, boys?*

I'm also five foot two. I need a step stool to reach some ceiling fan pulls, and yet I matched a six-foot-three boyfriend drink for drink. I also made genius decisions like skipping my dinner, trying to cut calories, because I was always scheming my way back to the size 4 dresses that hung in the back of my closet, like arrowheads from an ancient civilization.

Behold the risk factors for blacking out: a genetic predisposition to holding your liquor, drinking fast, and skipping meals. Oh, and one more: being female.

For a long time, blackouts were thought to be a guy thing. Of course, for a long time, drinking problems were thought to be a guy thing. But researchers now understand that women are more susceptible to blackouts than men. Alcohol metabolizes in our systems differently. Our bodies are smaller. Hormones can affect how quickly we get drunk. It's pure biology. Nature, as it turns out, insists on a few double standards.

The stories that men and women tell about their blackouts are different, too. All that alcohol can strip us down to our base drives. Our snarling, animal selves. I've heard countless tales of men waking up to find their faces bruised, their knuckles bloodied by some fit of unremembered violence.

The stories women tell are scary in another way. As Aaron White says, "When men are in a blackout, they do things to the world. When women are in a blackout, things are done to them."

I heard a saying once about drunks. Men wake up in jail cells, and women wake up in strangers' beds. It's not like that for everybody. But it was like that for me.

⁓

IT WAS SPRING 2010 when I heard the term "rape culture." I was 35, and editing a story for an online magazine, and strapped to my desk all the time, because I had to be.

"I honestly don't understand what this word means," I wrote to the author, in the blunt and slightly irritated language of a frazzled editor. The feminist blogosphere where she was a leading voice could get jargony, and I took a grammar snoot's delight in reminding writers their first duty was clarity.

"I bristled at the term at first, too," she responded, and sent me a link to a story called "Rape Culture 101." My eyes scanned a long list of ways that male sexual aggression was favored over women's safety, from movies that glamorize violent sex to the act of blaming a victim's behavior for her own rape.

It was one of those moments when I felt adrift from the feminist conversation. I'd only recently started calling myself a feminist. Writers at the magazine urged me to look past the baggage and the bickering around the term and address its core meaning: a belief that both sexes deserve equal opportunity and equal treatment. Back in high school, I'd been obsessed with the civil rights movement. My notebooks were emblazoned with Martin Luther King quotes. But it had never occurred to me to fight for my own gender. Maybe fishes don't know they're in a fishbowl, or maybe it's easier to identify another kid's short stick than to see the one you are holding.

Anyway, "rape culture" didn't track for me. Here I was, an editor at a magazine, run by a woman, working almost exclusively with female writers who wrote voluminously about female topics, and yet, we were being straitjacketed by a "rape culture"? I figured the term would sink back into the quiet halls of academic doublespeak. It spread like mad instead.

Over the next years, "rape culture" became one of the central issues around which smart, young women rallied online. And because this corner of the Internet was my neighborhood, the clamoring grew quite loud. A quick scan of personal essay pitches I received during this time: confronting my rapist; the rape I never reported; why won't my college students stop writing about their rapes?

In 2011, I watched the media coverage of "SlutWalks," a more provocative version of the old "Take Back the Night" candlelit vigils in which solemnness had been replaced by rage and a kind of punk aesthetic. Torn fishnets and f-bombs. The catalyst had been a police officer in Toronto suggesting that to avoid rape, women "should stop dressing like sluts." The response was a roar. *We can dress however the fuck we want.*

I marveled at their conviction. I mean, SlutWalks. How unambiguous is that? The organizers had clearly learned the lessons of social media and search engines, where language must have thrust. The participants were my kind of women—strong women, defiant women—though I felt a queasy mix of envy and alienation when I watched them. Maybe I missed the tigress growl of my own college years. Or maybe it's the curse of every generation to look at those behind them and wonder how they got so free.

The more I read about "rape culture," the more sense it made. Rape culture was a mind-set: the default view that a woman existed for a man's pleasure, that his desires somehow superseded her comfort in the world. I began to see it more and more. The construction workers at the Marcy stop on the JMZ train, who told me they wanted to titty-fuck me. *That was rape culture.* The guy on the subway who took a creepshot of my cleavage on his phone, making nausea spill over my insides. *That was rape culture.*

This younger generation seemed to understand—with a clarity I never possessed—that they didn't have to tolerate so much bullshit in the world. And I felt a little foolish, and a little complicit, that I spent so many years accepting this barbed wire as the way things are only to watch those women barreling into it, middle fingers raised.

By 2014, the term "rape culture" had made its way to *Time* magazine, which ran a cover story on campus sexual assault illustrated by a university sports banner emblazoned with the words "rape." Meanwhile, another media narrative was unfolding, this one about women and alcohol. CNN: "Why are more women drinking?" *USA Today*: "Binge drinking is a serious problem for women, girls."

To publicly connect these two narratives was to waltz into a very loaded minefield. Every once in a while, a columnist would come along and suggest women should drink less to avoid sexual assault. They contended if women didn't drink as much, they wouldn't be so vulnerable to danger. And those columnists were disemboweled upon arrival into the gladiator arena of public discourse. The response was a roar. *We can drink however the fuck we want.*

I understood the pushback. For way too long, women had been told how to behave. Women were sick of altering their behavior to please, to protect, to safeguard—while men peed their names across history. The new motto became "Don't tell us how to act, teach men not to rape." The entire conversation offered a needed corrective. Women are never to be blamed for getting raped. Women are never "asking for it" because of the way they dress or what they do.

And we women *can* drink however the fuck we want. I certainly did, and I'm not interested in taking away anyone's whiskey sour. But reading these salvos from entrenched battlegrounds made me feel kind of alone. In my life, alcohol often made the issue of consent very murky. More like an ink spill and nothing close to a clear line.

I knew why the women writing on these issues didn't want to acknowledge gray zones; gray zones were what the other side pounced on to gain ground. But I kept longing for a secret conversation, away from the pitchforks of the Internet, about how hard it was to match the clarity of political talking points to the complexity of life lived at last call.

Activism may defy nuance, but sex demands it. Sex was a complicated bargain to me. It was chase, and it was hunt. It was hide-and-seek, clash and surrender, and the pendulum could swing inside my brain all night: I will, no I won't; I should, no I can't.

I drank to drown those voices, because I wanted the bravado of a sexually liberated woman. I wanted the same freedom from internal conflict my male friends seemed to enjoy. So I drank myself to a place where I didn't care, but I woke up a person who cared enormously. Many yeses on Friday nights would have been nos on Saturday morning. My consent battle was in me.

I HAD WANTED alcohol to make me fearless. But by the time I'd reached my mid-30s, I was scared all the time. Afraid of what I'd said and done in blackouts. Afraid I would have to stop. Afraid of a life without alcohol, because booze had been my trustiest tool.

I needed alcohol to drink away the things that plagued me. Not just my doubts about sex. My self-consciousness, my loneliness, my insecurities, my fears. I drank away all the parts that made me human, in other words, and I knew this was wrong. My mind could cobble together a thousand PowerPoint presentations to keep me seated on a bar stool. But when the lights were off, and I lay very quietly in my bed, I knew: There was something fundamentally wrong about losing the narrative of my own life.

This book might sound like a satire of memoir. I'm writing about events I can't remember. But I remember so much *about* those blackouts. The blackouts leveled me, and they haunt me still. The blackouts showed me how powerless I had become. The nights I can't remember are the nights I can never forget.

PART ONE

ONE

THE BEER THIEF

I grew up in Dallas, Texas, wondering why. In the novels and buttery teen magazines I read, people of consequence lived in California and the East Coast, the glittering cities where a Jay Gatsby or a John Stamos might thrive. When I became obsessed with Stephen King books, I nursed fantasies of moving to Maine. Things happened in Maine, I told myself, never understanding *things happened in Maine* because Stephen King made them happen.

My father was an engineer for DuPont Chemical in 1970, but a crisis of conscience changed our family's entire trajectory. The environmental movement was getting started, and my dad wanted to be on the right side of history—cleaning up the planet, not pumping more toxins into it. He took a job with the burgeoning Environmental Protection Agency, which was opening up branches across the country, and in 1977, when I was three years old, we moved from a quaint Philadelphia suburb to the wilds of Dallas, a city so far removed from what we knew it might as well have been Egypt.

I've often wondered how much of my life would be different if we'd stayed where we sprouted. What part of my later troubles, my sense of estrangement could be traced back to this one simple set change—swapping the leafy and sun-dappled streets surrounding our apartment in Pennsylvania for the hot cement and swiveling highways of Big D?

My parents rented a small house on a busy street in the neighborhood with the best public school system in Dallas. The district was notorious for other things, too, though it took us a while to catch on: $300 Louis Vuitton purses on the shoulders of sixth graders, ski trips to second homes in Aspen or Vail, a line of BMWs and Mercedes snaking around the school entrance. Meanwhile, we drove a dented station wagon with a ceiling liner held up by staples and duct tape. We didn't have a chance.

Parents often try to correct the mistakes of their own past, but they end up introducing new errors. My father grew up in a public housing project in Detroit. My mother wondered what she might have achieved if she hadn't downshifted her intelligence through school. They wanted better opportunities for their two children. And so they moved into an area where all the kids went to college, an area so cloistered from the dangers of the big city it was known as the Bubble.

The neighborhood was a real slice of old-fashioned Americana: two-story redbrick homes and children selling lemonade on the corner. My brother and I rode our bikes to the shopping center a mile away to buy gummy worms and magic tricks, and we made As on our report cards, and we were safe. In fact, the only thief I ever knew was me.

I was a small-time crook. In middle school, I slipped lipstick and powder compacts into my pocket at the Woolworth's and smiled at the clerk as I passed. Every kid pushes boundaries, but something else was going on: Surrounded by a land of plenty, I couldn't shake the notion that what I had been given was not enough. So I "borrowed" clothes from other people's closets. I had an ongoing scam with the Columbia Record & Tape Club that involved changing the spelling of my name each time I joined. But the first thing I remember stealing was beer.

I was seven when I started sneaking sips of Pearl Light from half-empty cans left in the refrigerator. I would tiptoe into the kitchen in my cotton nightgown, and I would take two long pulls when no one was looking, and I would spin around the living room, giggling and knocking into furniture. A carnival ride of my very own.

Later, I would hear stories of girls this age discovering their bodies. A showerhead positioned between the thighs. The humping of a pillow after lights off. "You didn't do that?" people would ask, surprised and maybe a little bit sad for me.

I chased the pounding of my heart to other places. A bottle of cooking sherry under the sink. A bottle of Cointreau, screw top crusty with lack of use. But nothing was as good as beer. The fizz. The left hook of it. That wicked ka-pow.

In high school, girls would complain about beer—how gross and sour it was, how they could barely force themselves to drink it—and I was confused, as though they were bad-mouthing chocolate or summer vacation. The taste for beer was embroidered on my DNA.

❧

THE MOVE TO Dallas was hard on everyone, but it might have been toughest on my mom. She was catatonic for a week after our arrival. This was a woman who had traveled alone in Europe and was voted "most optimistic" in her high school class, but in the first days of our new life, she sat on the couch, unable to retrieve even a lampshade from the garage.

She was too overwhelmed. She'd never been so far from her big, noisy Irish brood, and though some part of her longed for distance, did she really want this much? My mother was also not what you'd call a Dallas type. She wore no makeup. She sewed her own empire-waist wedding dress, inspired by characters in Jane Austen books. And here she was at 33, with two kids, stranded in the land of rump-shaking cheerleaders and Mary Kay Cosmetics.

I was happy in those early years. At least, that's the story I'm told. I shimmied in the living room to show tunes. I waved to strangers. At bedtime, my mother would lean down close and tell me, "They said I could pick any girl baby I wanted, and I chose you." Her glossy chestnut hair, which she wore in a bun during the day, hung loose and swished like a horse's tail. I can still feel the cool slick of her hair through my fingers. The drape on my face.

I clung to her as long as I could. On the first day of kindergarten, I gripped her skirt and sobbed, but no amount of begging could stop the inevitable. Eden was over. And I was exiled to a table of loud, strange creatures with Play-Doh gumming their fingertips.

The first day of kindergarten was also a rocky transition for me, because it was the last day I breast-fed. Yes, I was one of those kids who stayed at the boob well past the "normal" age, a fact that caused me great embarrassment as I grew older. My cousins dangled the tale over my head like a wriggly worm, and I longed to scrub the whole episode from my record. (A bit of blackout wished for but never granted.)

The way my mother tells it, she tried to wean me earlier, but I threw tantrums and lashed out at other children in frustration. And I asked very nicely. *Just once more, Mommy. Just one more time.* So she let me crawl back up to the safest spot on earth, and she didn't mind. My mother believed kids develop on their own timelines, and a child like me simply needed a few bonus rounds. She wanted to be a softer mother than the one she had. The kind who could intuit her children's needs, although I can't help wondering if I was intuiting hers.

These were the hardest years of my parents' marriage. Nothing was turning out the way my mother expected—not her husband, not her life. But she and I continued in our near-umbilical connection, as diapers turned to big-girl pants and long-term memories formed on my developing mind. Was she wrong to let me cling like this? Did she set up unrealistic expectations that the world would bend to my demands? Was this a lesson in love—or codependence? I don't know what role, if any, my protracted breast-feeding plays in my drinking story. But I know that whatever I got from my mother in the perfect little cocoon of ours was something I kept chasing for a long, long time.

I was in first grade when my mom went back to school, and much of the following years are defined by her absence. She disappeared in phases, oxygen slowly leaking from the room, until one day I looked around to find my closest companion had been relegated to cameo appearances on nights and weekends.

She became a therapist, the go-to profession for wounded hearts. She wanted to work with children—abused children, neglected children, which had the unintended consequence of pulling her away from her own. She cut her long brown hair into a no-nonsense '80s do. She stored her ponytail in a hatbox on a high shelf in her bedroom closet, and sometimes I would pull it down, just to run my fingers over it again.

EVEN THOUGH I was seven when I first stole beer, I was six when I first tasted it. My father took care of me and my brother in the evenings, and he spent most of the hours in a squishy chair in the living room, watching news reports of weather and death. I often saw him with his eyes closed, but he swore he wasn't napping, which made me curious where he had gone, which alternate reality was better than ours.

He nursed one beer each night. Sometimes two. He poured the beer into a glass, and I could smell the hops dancing in the air as I passed. Few scents crackle my nerve endings like beer. As gorgeous as campfire, as unmistakable as gasoline.

I sidled up to him. *Can I have a sip?*

Just one. I placed my nose in the glass, and I could feel stardust on my face.

I don't know if parents still let their kids taste beer, but it wasn't uncommon at the time. The bitterness was supposed to turn us off the stuff, but that one sip lit a fuse in me that burned for decades.

My parents weren't big drinkers back then, but thirst ran in our bloodlines. My mother's Irish heritage requires no explanation. My father's background is Finnish, a nationality fabled for its shyness and its love of booze (two qualities that are not unrelated). To be both Irish and Finnish is to be bred for drinking—doomed to burst into song and worry later what everyone thought about it.

My dad was self-conscious like me. He was self-conscious about his ears, which he thought stood out funny, and the vitiligo that looked like spilled bleach across his arms and shins. He was a handsome man, with a beaming smile, but he carried himself like someone who didn't want to be noticed. He wore a lot of beige.

My father's EPA office was in the flashy downtown skyscraper where J. R. Ewing swindled his fortunes on the TV show *Dallas*. But the two men couldn't have been further apart. My father was a diligent government worker who scanned our bills at Steak and Ale to flag any item accidentally left off the tab. He took me to a movie every Saturday, and he let me choose the film (a luxury no second child forgets), but he was so anxious about arriving on time we often showed up before the previous movie had ended. We'd linger in the lobby for 20 minutes, the two of us sitting on carpeted stair steps, not talking.

As much as my father was there during my childhood, he was also not there. He had an introversion common to Finns, and to engineers. He avoided eye contact. If he was growing up today, I'm curious what a psychiatrist would make of him. He had a boyhood habit of stimming, rocking back and forth to soothe himself. In his 20s, he had a compulsive blinking tic. In his middle age, he kept a notebook listing every winning Dallas lotto number, recorded in his careful, geometrically precise block lettering. A futile attempt at charting randomness.

Perhaps these were coping mechanisms of a childhood harsher than mine. His father was sent to a mental institution when my dad was 15—a breakdown brought on by mental illness, drinking, or both. But most of my dad's past, like my dad himself, was a mystery to me. All I knew was that my father was not like those loud, wisecracking fathers on sitcoms who tousled your hair and tickled you till you snorted. He communicated in his own rhythms. If I said, "I love you, Daddy," he would sometimes pat my head and say, "OK. Thanks." So I learned that fathers were very loyal and dependable people who existed behind glass.

My mother was full of passion and conversation. I sometimes marveled these two people ever came together, but I was charmed by tales of their courtship. In lieu of an engagement ring, my father gave her money to study in Germany, an act of gentle nonconformity and global discovery that shaped my worldview. But at night, in our cramped house, their fights curled like smoke underneath their bedroom door. And as tender as my mother could be, an Irish fire lurked in her, too. I could hear her voice each night, bitten by frustration. The tone that always made the veins on the side of her neck stand up like cords. *Why can't you do this right, John? Why can't you listen, John?*

For a while, my brother and I were allies on this battleground. Josh was my hero, a swashbuckling little boy who could find excitement in any dusty corner. He turned blankets into royal capes and wicker chairs into spaceships from a galaxy far, far away. He was four and a half years older than me, with a precocious mind forever solving the Rubik's Cube of how the world worked. Of course, he solved his actual Rubik's Cube. I gave up, and changed the stickers.

I didn't realize it, but Josh had a rough entry to school, too. A Yankee boy dropped into a part of the world where kids were still fighting the Civil War. The brainiac skills that wowed his younger sister were useless on the football field, where Texas boys proved their mettle. And by the time he entered middle school, our shared excursions had turned into his solo journeys: onto the clunky personal computer he won in a radio contest, into the J. R. R. Tolkien books crinkled and dog-eared with devotion. I wanted to follow him into those exotic boylands, but he started closing doors in my face. *Get out. Go away.*

I got my own room. Pink walls, red carpet, a Strawberry Shortcake explosion. And in this private universe, where no one could criticize me, I was the star of every show. My fantasy worlds were dominated by girls like me, discovering their own power. I was Sandy, in the last scene of *Grease*, strutting in hot pants and causing a bulge in every man's heart. I was plucky Orphan Annie, rescued by a billionaire she saved right back. I was Coco, fan-kicking her way through the cafeteria in *Fame*.

Fame. I wanted it more than anything. If you were famous, nothing hurt. If you were famous, everyone loved you. In fifth grade, I would start plastering my walls with teen pinups—Prince Charming in the form of a soft boy with a popped collar—and I became fixated on celebrity and glamour, those twin instruments of escape.

But before that, there was the beer.

OUR PEARL LIGHT lived in 12-packs resting on the floor to the right of our cream-colored Kenmore fridge. Reaching inside that cardboard box gave me a bad thrill, like sinking my hands into a vat of warm wax. All that carbonated joy rumbling around my fingertips.

My mother often stored a half-empty can in the fridge to drink over the course of an evening. She would stuff a rubber stopper that looked like a lime wedge in the mouth.

This was 1981, and we were always dreaming up new ways to keep our carbonated beverages from going flat. My mother's older sister informed us if you crunched the big plastic soda bottle before you tightened the cap, you could preserve the carbonation. Our soda bottles looked like they'd taken a flight on an airplane: sunken bellies, cratered at each side. The rubber stoppers were part of this scheme to prolong shelf life, though they never worked. The fizz leaked out anyway. You would come back to your can the next day and find it flat and syrupy. Eventually those lime wedges ended up in a kitchen drawer alongside twisties and dead batteries, another failed experiment in fighting the way of the world.

But when I began stealing sips of my mother's beer, we still had faith in the lime wedges. I would pop that sucker out and take a few glugs—not enough to be obvious but enough to get melty inside—and I would put the can back exactly where I found it. On the door side, next to the raspberry jam. On the top shelf, beside the cantaloupe, logo facing the back.

I didn't do this every day. I didn't even do this every month. It was a special-occasion indulgence. A splurge. But I did it for many years, as the 12-pack grew into the economy 18-pack from Sam's Wholesale and cotton nightgowns turned into striped pajama bottoms and Duran Duran T-shirts.

Sometimes I went too far, because the beer was like a wave I wanted to keep crashing into. I would misjudge a few swigs and realize the can was nearly empty. I couldn't put my mother's Pearl Light back in the fridge with nothing but backwash in it.

So I had to drain that can and pop open a new one, drinking it down to the original level, which made me woozy with rainbows. I would take the empty back to my bedroom and shove it behind the foldout chair in the corner until I could slip out to the alley and dump it in someone else's trash.

It's odd I was never caught. Sometimes my mother noticed her beer lower than when she left it, but she wrote it off to a fluke of memory. And my father kept his eyes on my brother—who was, literally, a Boy Scout. Any con man depends on people looking in the wrong direction, but perhaps nothing worked more to my advantage than gender bias. Nobody thought a little girl would steal beer.

I WAS IN fourth grade when I began to realize my family might be out of our league in the neighborhood. One afternoon, a friend's father was driving me home when he asked, "Does your dad *rent* that house?"

"I think so," I said.

"Innnnteresting," he said, in a way that told me it was not interesting but shameful.

There are moments you can taste your difference, like copper on your tongue. I began lying after that. Little lies, lies no one could catch. *Yes, I've been to Aspen. No, that's not our car. Absolutely I've been accepted to the School of Performing Arts in New York.* When people asked where my father worked, I named the building but not the profession. "He's a banker?" And I said, "I guess so." Banking was a power career. Banking meant money.

Our home was on a major artery through the neighborhood, where cars zipped past all day long, forcing us to keep the blinds drawn at all times. I started using the back door to come and go. I didn't want strangers to see me and know the dinky rental house was ours.

My mother had become embarrassing to me as well. She listened exclusively to classical music and hummed conspicuously in public. She had a therapeutic chattiness that felt like a doctor's probe. "How do you feel about that, Sarah? Tell me more." God forbid we pass a mother with a baby in the grocery store. She had to download the entire backstory. How cute, and how special, and blah to the blah. And my mother didn't assemble herself like those kicky mothers of the PTA, with their frosted hair and ropy gold necklaces. She wasn't bad-looking. But didn't she realize how much prettier she'd look with some eye shadow?

Even my brother was a frustration. "You're Josh's sister?" the teachers would say on the first day of class, eyebrows arched with delight. But no matter what high score I made, his had been higher. Don't even try, kid. Someone already won this race.

I got a crazy idea I'd be rescued from this unspecial life. Surely I was meant for more. In the customer service area of JC Penney, while waiting for my mom to complete some transaction, I watched women file in, hoping each new one in a smart dress suit was a fairy godmother carrying my new fate. I'd catch her glance as she passed, hoping she'd see the star pattern in my eyes. *Oh, it's you. I found you.* Does every child have this fantasy—or just the sad ones?

I was very torn about my mother. She never abandoned me, but I felt abandoned in some hyperbolic childhood way, the same way I deemed it a mortal sin I never got a Barbie Dream House. A thing known but never discussed: *Your mother needs some time to herself.* I learned to tread lightly during the hectic workweek. If you tapped her shoulder at the wrong time, she could snap. She was spending more and more time at the piano, the instrument she yearned to play as a girl, but her mother never allowed it, and now I had to pay the price. I wanted to push the plunky contraption in the nearest lake. I despised having her so near and far away at once. But on the weekends, I would curl up in her big king-size bed and let her read me stories, and I would mold my body alongside hers till we were two interlocking puzzle pieces.

My mother wanted badly to make me an active reader, a lover of literature like her, but I remained weirdly stubborn on this count. *Little Women* wasn't doing it for me. I gravitated toward stories of troubled kids. Judy Blume. *The Outsiders.* But I never fully sparked to imaginary worlds until I found Stephen King.

Everyone knew Stephen King wasn't for children. But that was perfect, because I no longer wanted to be a child. My older cousins had introduced me to his books, which were like a basement I wasn't supposed to enter, but I creaked open the door anyway. Whatever you do, *do not go inside.* So I tiptoed forward, heart like a kick drum. Not much else could grab my attention after I'd felt breath that close to my face. Not the stuffy novels assigned in English class. Not the lions and the witches and the wardrobes the other kids read in their free time. I didn't need those talking woodland creatures or those magic carpet rides.

Because the magic carpet arrived when I plucked the lime wedge out of the Pearl Light and poured the golden liquid down my throat. That's when the living room rug levitated, and the world tilted upside down, and I began to convulse with laughter. Why was I laughing anyway? What was so funny? But there is ecstasy in the room you are not supposed to enter, the room no one knows about. Ecstasy when everyone is gone and still you are held.

It was my aunt Barbara's idea for Josh and me to spend summers with her family in Kalamazoo. I was eight when she offered to take us while my mom completed her schoolwork, an older sister's act of generosity and superiority: Part "Let me help you while you're struggling," part "Let me show you how it's done."

My aunt and uncle Joe lived on a peaceful cul-de-sac with a big sloping hill out front. They had a waterbed. A big puffy couch with footrests that lifted when you turned the wooden crank. A giant console TV that doubled as floor furniture. Their home was like walking into a time capsule branded "1982."

My mother had strict limits on our television and sugar intake. Debates in the cereal aisle were like trying to get a bill through Congress. But my aunt pooh-poohed that hippie nonsense. At her place, we lived on Cap'n Crunch and Little Debbie snack cakes. I lay around in my nightgown till noon, watching game shows and soap operas. At night, we gathered around the big TV to watch prime-time dramas and R-rated movies.

Josh and I had three cousins—Joey, Kimberley, and Scotty—and I was the youngest in our group. To be the littlest in that gang was a mixed blessing. It was to be hoisted on the shoulders of new adventure at the same time I was blamed for someone else's farts. We filmed our own version of *Star Wars*, directed and produced by my brother, and I was dying to be Princess Leia. Instead, he cast me as R2D2. I didn't even get the dignity of lines to memorize. Just a series of random bleeps and bloops.

The part of Princess Leia went to Kimberley, a cute tomboy with feathered bangs, though production broke down when she failed to show on set. Kimberley wasn't obedient like me. Her response to boys who thought they ruled the world was a sarcastic eye roll. She was Josh's age, but she actually preferred my company, which probably felt like having a little sister and a disciple at once. She let me tag along to Crossroads Mall and taught me things about sex never mentioned in my mother's "when two people love each other" lectures.

She tried to make me tougher. The universe had made me soft, too quick to sniffle, and she saw it as her duty to make me better prepared. We used to play this game.

"I'm going to plant a garden," she would say, running her fingers along the tender skin of my inner arm. Her nails were like a caress at first, a tickle of sorts, but as the game progressed, the friction intensified. "I'm going to rake my garden," she would say, digging into my skin and scraping, leaving pink trails. "I'm going to plant seeds in the garden," she would say, twisting up a corkscrew of flesh between thumb and forefinger. What a strange game, a femmy version of "uncle." Girls can be so sideways with their aggression. Why not just punch each other and get it over with? Instead, we inch into the bizarre eroticism of inflicting and accepting each other's pain. I could never beat Kimberley—but I gnashed my teeth, gulped down my tears, and tried.

I wanted to be like her: tough and foxy. I wanted to borrow her brassiness. *What are you looking at? Who gave you permission to look at me?* How exciting to barge through the world, never apologizing for your place in it but demanding everyone else's license and registration.

But the summer of 1984 wasn't like the ones before it. I was nearly 10 years old, and Kimberley was 14. When I arrived, she greeted me in a tight magenta leopard-print tank top. Her eyes were lined with electric blue, and she wore hypnotic pink discs in her ears that swirled when she shifted. Men watched her as she crossed a room. She didn't smile much anymore.

She'd transformed, like Olivia Newton-John in the last scene in *Grease*, though she wasn't nearly as bubbly and fun. I was afraid of that leopard-print shirt. It was a costume change I didn't request. But on afternoons when Kimberley was gone, I would slip it off the hanger and onto the frightening curves of my own body, and I would admire myself in the mirror, enjoying the electricity of high school before I'd even started fifth grade.

SOMETHING ELSE TERRIBLE happened that year.

A few days into fifth grade, I was on the living room floor with my legs splayed open like any girl who is young and unencumbered. Mom and I were laughing about something, but she went silent when she saw it: a dime-size dot of rust on the crotch of my favorite shorts.

There was a rush to the bathroom. And an inspection over the toilet. And my mother's hands, smoothed along my ruddy cheeks.

"This is all very natural," she said, although we both knew that wasn't true. I'd just turned ten. I stared at the drain in the bathtub and watched my childhood go down it.

My precocious puberty had been coming on for a while, but the changes had been manageable. When breasts bubbled up on my chest in fourth grade, I smushed them down again under heavy cable-knit sweaters. When hair began to appear on my privates, unwelcome as the first whiskers of a werewolf, I ran my mother's razor along the skin to keep it smooth and untarnished. But bleeding once a month required a new level of hiding.

My fifth-grade teacher called my mother at home one night after becoming concerned about my slouch. "Sarah should be proud of her body," she said. "She's blessed to have such a shape." What the hell? She was supposed to be grading my math quizzes, not my posture. Until that moment, it hadn't occurred to me that adults might also have opinions about my body, which meant everyone did, and I hated feeling so powerless. You could hunch and smother yourself, you could shove all your shame into unlit places, but somehow, some way, some gray-haired lady could still spot your secrets from across the room.

My mother came into my room later that night. She thought it might be time to shop for a bra. And I tried to be patient with her, but didn't she understand? That was the worst idea in the world. Fifth grade was a torture chamber for any girl who dared to confirm her development. Boys would sneak up behind me and snap my bra. Girls would whisper behind my back. I might as well show up to school wearing a bull's-eye on each areola. I might as well take a Sharpie and draw an arrow to my crotch: *now bleeding.*

So my mother smoothed my hair and kissed my forehead. My mother's hand is still my favorite hand.

That was the year I started encouraging girls at sleepovers to sneak sips from the liquor cabinet. I wanted to make them tough, too. And I liked playing ringleader in our coterie of spelling bee champions. I taught them dirty jokes and cusswords I'd learned from watching Eddie Murphy films at my cousins' house. I got the genius idea to pass notes in class and archive them in a plastic index cardholder inside our desks, which is such a boneheaded girl thing to do. It's not enough to break the rules. Apparently you need to scrapbook the evidence.

We returned from P.E. one afternoon to find our teacher sitting behind a desk piled with a mountain of our misdeeds. I was a real show-off in the notes. I called her a bitch. I talked about how goddamn nosy she was. It was a grudge I'd nursed since she had called my house.

"I really thought you liked me," she said.

"I *do* like you," I said, because what was I going to say? She was the one who started it?

Every one of those girls got grounded except me. My parents didn't believe in grounding.

I was in bed when my mom came into my room. She had one of the notes in her hand, and I hated that she was seeing me like that.

"Help me understand why you're so angry," she said.

But I wasn't the one smashing dishes and arguing with my father after the kids went to bed. My parents' fights were bad that year. I turned up the radio to drown out the sound. I listened to the Top 10 countdown every night, and I tracked the movements of songs by Madonna, and Michael Jackson, and Prince the way other children might count sheep.

"I'm not angry," I told her.

"Then what are you?" she asked.

I thought maybe I was bad. A lot of crazy things were building up inside me, and the more they accumulated, the stronger the suspicion that I was messed up and wrong. I shrugged my shoulders. Tears dripped down my cheeks.

"I'm sorry," my mother said, pulling me into her, and I was so confused. My family made no sense to me. I had screwed up, but somehow she was apologizing.

I GOT DRUNK for the first time in the summer of my sixth-grade year. Kimberley was 16 and working at an arcade so epic it was called Star World. Dark rooms lit by neon, full of clinking machines and 25-cent shots at redemption. A bar for people who can't drink yet.

My self-consciousness had become overpowering by then. I couldn't stop dreaming about those shaggy-haired boys playing Galaga, but words were staple-gunned to the back of my throat. I hung around the arcade all day, but I never said a word. Someone actually asked Kimberley, "Is your cousin mute?"

The staff of Star World threw an end-of-summer party in a house by the lake. For the first two hours, I stayed in my usual spot on the sidelines. Teenagers played quarters on the table and drank potions I understood to be off-limits: peach schnapps and orange juice, rum and Coke.

But then the pudgy assistant manager handed me a beer. He must have felt sorry for me: Kimberley's little cousin, watching from the benches again. Or maybe he had reached the euphoric point in your buzz when stupid ideas seem brilliant. Let's pee our names in the snow. Let's get the dog drunk. He grabbed a Budweiser out of the fridge and handed it to me, like he was sliding me a winning lottery ticket. *Hey, you're cool, right?*

I was two weeks shy of my twelfth birthday, but I had been practicing for this moment for years. I knew how to pop open the can with a gratifying *pfffffft* that sprayed like the lightest afternoon shower on my face. I knew how to tolerate the zap on my tongue and the way my glands squeezed like a fist. I knew how to sip, and I knew how to glug. Yes, sir. I was cool.

I drank the beer. Then I drank another. And the evening began to glow in my veins. Words rolled out to me on red carpets. The perfect comeback. The fastest burn. And I kept drinking: a syrupy mixed drink, a shot of clear liquor like a grenade down my gullet. That shit tasted awful, but who cared? I was transformed. Pierced by divine light. Filled by a happiness I'd longed for all my life.

I threw up seven times. Hunched over the toilet, Kimberley at my side. The Star World manager tucked me into bed in a room upstairs. "You're too young to be drinking like this," he said. He was a sweet guy, with a hangdog face, and I nodded in agreement. He was wise and ancient, twice as old as me. He was 22.

The next morning I was so shaky I could barely force blueberry yogurt in my mouth. And Kimberley was asking me weird questions. "Do you remember when you took your pants off last night?" And I laughed, because I knew that couldn't have happened. I wouldn't even undress in Kimberley's room when she was there. I sure as hell didn't strip off my clothes at a Star World party.

But she had the unsmiling voice of a state's witness. "You sat at the bottom of the steps, crying, and you said everyone loved me more than you. You don't remember that?"

I did not.

It's such a savage thing, to lose your memory, but the crazy part is, it doesn't hurt one bit. A blackout doesn't sting, or stab, or leave a scar when it robs you. Close your eyes and open them again. That's what a blackout feels like.

The blackout scattered whatever pixie dust still remained from the night before, and I was spooked by the lost time. I had no idea this could happen. You could be present and not there at all. Those first few drinks gave me hope for escape. But I knew from Stephen King stories how hope could boomerang on a person and what looked like an exit door turned out to be the mouth of a more dangerous maze.

So I swore I'd never drink like that again. And I kept the promise for many years. I kept drinking, but not *like that*. Never *like that*. I assured myself it was a first-time drinker's mistake. Instead, it was a blueprint.

TWO

STARVED

One of the curious aspects of middle school is how extra-ordinary the pain feels, even when the affliction is quite mundane. The wrong pair of jeans, your unpronounceable last name, a paper wad thrown by a popular boy that hit your back during an assembly. *Has anyone ever suffered like this?* My mother used to tell me all kids were struggling. Even the bullies. "It's such a tough time for everyone," she would say, and get a tsk-tsk look, like she was talking about Ethiopia. A nice perspective, I suppose. But I was pretty sure my unhappiness was worse than everyone else's.

In sixth grade, I walked home alone every day. In the quiet hours before my brother returned from football and my parents returned from work, I rooted around our cabinets for new kinds of comfort. Graham crackers. Chunks of cheddar cheese melted in the microwave for exactly seven seconds, the moment the sides began to slump. Sips of occasional beer weren't enough anymore. I needed the numbing agents of sugar and salt.

Becoming a binge eater in a house like mine wasn't easy. You

had to get creative. My mother bought natural, oily peanut butter, but if you swirled a spoonful with molasses, you had something approaching a Reese's. Four tubes of cake icing sat on the
fourth shelf of the pantry, and I squirted a dollop in my mouth
each day.

But my new comfort also brought a new pain. "You're getting
fat," my brother told me one day, as I watched *Oprah* on the
couch. He and I didn't speak much anymore. He stuck to his
room and his Judas Priest. But he had an older sibling's homing
device for sore spots. "Fat" was the meanest word you could call
a girl. The absolute worst thing in the world.

My first diet started in seventh grade. My cafeteria lunch
shrank to iceberg lettuce dribbled with low-cal ranch dressing.
I loaded up on Diet Cokes. Three, four a day. After school, I
grape-vined to Kathy Smith's aerobic workout. I confined myself
to frozen Lean Cuisine dinners. Cheese pizza. Cheese cannel-
loni. Cheese lasagna. (The same three ingredients, rolled up in
different shapes.) The diet craze of the 1980s was a nationwide
tornado that left leg warmers and V-hip leotards in its wake. Even
my food co-op mother bought a book listing calorie counts, and
I memorized those entries like Bible passages. I couldn't tell you
much about John 3:16, but I knew Blueberry Muffin: 426.

The misery of calorie restriction is well documented, but
what people rarely mention is that it's also a bit fun. How much
hunger can I tolerate? How much joy can I withhold? What a
perverse pleasure, to be in charge of your own pain.

My extreme dieting became a power struggle with my mother,
just like the extreme amount of Wet N Wild makeup I wore or
the extreme number of sitcoms I watched every afternoon. *I* was
the dish thrower in our house now. The good part about weight
obsession, though, is how it bonded me with other girls. Quite a

few of us were sweating in unitards by then. Two of my friends told me about lying in bed one afternoon in their bathing suits, circling trouble spots on each other's body with a permanent marker. And when I heard that story, I thought: *That is love.*

⌒⌒⌒

BY EIGHTH GRADE, I had discovered a surprisingly dependable revenue stream for adulation. I wrote morbid little tales inspired by Stephen King books. Teachers and classmates cooed over my twisted imagination and PSAT vocabulary. Writing made school an opportunity instead of a fear parade. Of course, English was my favorite subject.

I met one of my first great loves in my English class. Jennifer had big brown eyes, long brown hair, and a bohemian beaded necklace that suggested an older sister who taught her about Pink Floyd. She sat directly in front of me, and we bonded over our liberal politics and *Helter Skelter,* required reading for curious teens dabbling in darkness.

One day she slipped me a note on a torn piece of paper. *Do you want to spend the night on Friday?* Later, she told me she spent the entire class holding the tiny scrap of hope in her hands, trying to talk herself into passing it my way.

That Friday night, we sat in her bedroom and ate an entire gallon of Blue Bell ice cream. That's how nervous and excited we were. We swapped stories of our own personal hells and discovered they weren't so personal after all. Is there any bonding agent like shared pain? We spent most Friday nights together after that.

I thought I had delicate sensibilities, but Jennifer was the most sensitive girl I'd ever met. We once passed a bird with a broken wing as we walked to NorthPark Mall. He was tipped over on the sidewalk near the highway, claws scrambling for purchase, and she scooped him up in her hands and redirected us back to her house, where she nestled him in a shoe box padded with cotton balls. I just wanted to go to Limited Express.

"You can't go around rescuing any dumb bird," I said to her in a tone I'd borrowed from Kimberley. My babysitting money was heavy in my pocket, and I was itching to turn my bounty into a bubble skirt.

I was the dominant in our duo, but in the green-carpeted hallways of middle school, we were equals. Two artsy honors kids, stranded in the vast flyover territory between cheerleader and nerd, and drawn to both coasts. We wrote each other notes every day, which tracked the movements of boys we liked as though we were anthropologists in the bush. ("Claude was wearing a red shirt today. He sat in a seat close to the door.") We folded the notes into simple origami shapes, and I kept every one she gave me in a Payless ShoeSource box in my closet. I liked to watch those notes pile up, a tangible measure of my value to another human. The notes were creamy with praise, as if self-esteem were a present you could give another person. *You are beautiful and sweet. I love you so much. You are the best friend I ever had.* So much clinging and drama. We sounded like parting lovers fleeing the Nazis, not two kids bored in American History.

We bought silver best friend rings from James Avery, the equivalent of engagement rings in our junior high. Flashing that ring meant you belonged to someone. And if we couldn't belong to the boys we liked, then at least we could belong to each other. The ring was two hands entwined so you couldn't tell where one hand ended and the other one began, a fitting symbol for our enmeshment. We were BFFs, almost sisters. But then high school came along—and our unraveling began.

I arrived in ninth grade eager to catch the eye of some

upperclassman, but it was Jennifer they saw. They scooped her up only to drop her again, but at least they knew she was alive. The baby fat had melted off her round cheeks, and she wore tight miniskirts displaying her long, shapely legs. She developed a scary case of anorexia that year. If she chewed a stick of sugar-free gum, she would run around the block to burn calories. And I knew she was acting crazy, but I was so jealous of how much more successful her eating disorder was than mine.

It was also dawning on me, with horror, that I was short. To some girls, being short meant "petite" and "dainty." To me, it meant being "squat" and "puny." Height was authority. Height was glamour. I knew from magazines that supermodels were at least five nine but I flatlined at five two, while Jennifer rose to an attractive five seven, and I grew accustomed to tilting my head upward as I spoke. Jennifer once caught me climbing onto their kitchen countertop to reach a high shelf. "Aww, that's cute," she said.

"No, it's not," I snapped at her. What was so adorable about a person whose body had been cheated?

On Friday nights, in her bedroom, we didn't discuss these frictions. We giggled and gossiped. Jennifer stole beer from her father's stash of Schaefer Light for me. I would drink it while we talked, letting the alcohol work out the kinks in my system, the part of me that couldn't stop staring at Jennifer's thighs and hating her for them.

Jennifer didn't like beer, but she had other vices. She liked to sneak out the back window of the house in the middle of the night and take out her parents' Oldsmobile. We glided down the streets of her neighborhood in that gray boat, our hearts booming louder than the radio, and then coaxed it back into her driveway. I could not have cared less about driving a car. But I played accomplice to her minor crime, same as she did for me, because we were good girlfriends like that. Always taking care of the other one's needs.

⁓

I WAS A sophomore when the whispers began. *Did you know so-and-so drinks? Did you know so-and-so can buy?* Nobody needed to explain what the person was drinking and which substance they could buy. It was like the teenage version of the mafia. You just knew.

Ours was a conservative religious community. At pep rallies, a "prayer warrior" spoke before the big game. Youth ministers from the behemoth Presbyterian Church milled around the cafeteria at lunch. Popular girls wore silver cross necklaces and signed their notes "In His Grip." But these kids were destined for the sanctioned debauch of fraternities and sororities, so high school was a slow seduction from one team to the other. I kept a running list in my head—who had gone to the devil's side.

For a while, drinking was an underground society. I would show up to a fancy house on the old-money side of town, where the parents had gone on vacation (Aspen? Vail?), and I'd end up in some deep conversation with a stoner from my Racquet Sports class. When people asked later how we'd become friends, I had to remain vague. *Oh, you know, some thing.* Drinking forged unlikely connections. It dissolved the social hierarchies that had tyrannized us for so long. Like a play-at-home version of *The Breakfast Club.*

Jennifer had started to drink, too. Grape wine coolers and sugary concoctions. Girlie drinks. She had taken up with an older crowd, the ones who smoked on the corner across from the school. I hung out with the drama kids and slipped my best friend's ring in a drawer; that was baby stuff now.

Theater was my new love. My energy shifted from academics to performance. I appeared in every play. I joined not one but two choirs. I had to keep my weight down for the stage, which meant at parties, I never allowed myself more than three Coors Lights, 102 calories each. My body obsession was not pretty, but at least it kept my drinking in check.

My new companion was Stephanie, a fellow drama geek. She and I took long aerobic walks after school. Afterward, we smoked Marlboro Lights at the Black-Eyed Pea while picking at our vegetable plates and talking about our future fabulous selves in New York. God, we had to get out of this town.

Stephanie was blond, poised, and gorgeous. She was also five nine. She actually glided down the hallway, her full lips in a pout, the indifferent stare of the runway on her face. I'd known Stephanie since sixth grade, when she was a sweet and bookish beanpole, but in our sophomore year, her body announced its exceptional status: boobs, graceful arms, legs to forever. Guys came up to me in class to ask if I knew her, as though she were already famous.

So much of high school is a competition for resources—attention from boys, praise from peers and teachers, roles in the school play—and it's a dicey gamble to position yourself alongside one of the most breathtaking girls in the class. I'm not sure if this shows masochism on my part, or grandiosity, or both. I've never been devoured by envy like I was with Stephanie. To watch her enter a room in knee-high leather boots, her long, straight hair trailing behind her was to practically taste my peasant status. But I also saw her as my kind. I wrote my notes to her now. They were in the form of Top Ten lists, because we worshipped David Letterman and needed to hone our joke-writing skills. The path seemed obvious. Go to college, then join the cast of *Saturday Night Live*.

I never meant to leave Jennifer behind. There was never a ceremony in which Jennifer handed a baton to Stephanie for the next leg of the relay, but female friendships can be a swap like this. Only a certain number of runners on the track at once.

I threw a hotel party with my new theater companions and invited Jennifer. By the time I got to the La Quinta, she was already wasted. She began spewing compliments in a dangerously slushy state. *You're so pretty. I miss you.* She stirred up all kinds of drama when she made out with a friend's boyfriend. The next day I could barely look her in the face.

"What is wrong with you?" I asked her as we drove away from the hotel. "Have you completely lost your mind?"

She didn't answer, because she couldn't remember. She had blacked out and—just like we both would in years to come—poured herself into whatever hands wandered her way.

That night fractured our friendship for good. Jennifer graduated a year early. And I got a boyfriend. I belonged to him now.

❧

I WAS A junior in high school when my parents finally busted me. I came home from school to find a half-empty 12-pack of Coors Light sitting in front of my bedroom door, with a note that read: *We'll talk about this when your dad gets home.*

The beer was a gift from my boyfriend, Miles, a funny guy with delicate features and an equal fluency in Monty Python and David Bowie. He gave me the Coors Light for my sixteenth birthday, along with a $25 gift certificate to the Gap, a reflection of my hierarchy of needs at the time. I stored the 12-pack in the back of my closet, underneath dirty clothes, and I would sneak a can out of it from time to time. Three were smuggled in my woven bucket purse and slurped with friends before a dance.

Another was shoved between my cleavage underneath a mock turtleneck as I paraded past my father in the middle of the day, just to prove I could. I drank one of them on a lazy Saturday, sipping it in my bedroom, because I liked the casualness of the gesture, a high school girl playing college.

But my clever ruse fell apart when my mother dug through my closet to recover a shirt I'd borrowed. She couldn't miss the silver glint of contraband in the dim light.

I couldn't predict how my parents were going to react to this discovery. They were so different than other parents. Half my friends' folks had divorced by then. Jennifer's father lived in an undecorated apartment across town. Stephanie's mother moved the girls into a duplex, while her dad began a slow drift that would take him out of her life completely. All those shiny, happy families, splintered into custody arrangements and second marriages. And yet, somehow, my parents stayed together. My mom was happier, less volatile now—a result of her intensive therapy, four times a week. We used to joke that for the price of a new home, we got a healthy mother. My parents may have argued their way through my elementary school years, but by the time they sat me down in the living room that night, they were united.

"Your father and I would like to know where you got this beer," my mother said.

I wasn't sure how to spin this episode. How much reality could they handle? I'd been drinking for years at this point with such assurance that playing dumb would be an insult to my pride. At the same time, my folks were on the naive end, and most of what they knew about underage drinking came from 60 Minutes–style segments where teenagers wound up in hospitals. Of course, things really did spin out of control at some of our parties, and even I was uncomfortable with the level of oblivion. A friend had recently crashed his car while driving drunk. I was worried about him—but it gave me an idea.

"I know it's upsetting to find something like this," I told my parents. "But what you don't realize is that I'm holding the beer for a friend, who has a drinking problem."

I hated lying to them. They were so earnest. I felt like I was kicking a cocker spaniel in the teeth. But the lie was necessary, the same way I had to tell them Miles and I were "just talking" during all those late nights we drove around in his 1972 Chevy Nova. The lies allowed me to continue doing what I wanted, but they also shielded my folks from guilt and fear. Kids lie to their parents for the same reason their parents lie to them. We're all trying to protect each other.

My dad wasn't quite convinced. "Look me in the eye, and tell me that's not your beer."

I leveled my gaze with his. "That's not my beer," I said, without a tic of doubt in my voice. And I thought: *Holy shit. Is it really going to be this easy?*

It was. I wasn't displaying any of the classic distress signals. I was on the honor roll. I had a boyfriend everyone liked. I beat out Stephanie for the lead in the senior play. On Sundays, I ran the nursery at my parents' progressive, gay-friendly church, and I even landed my first job, at a center for Children of Alcoholics, because I was the sort of kid who helped other kids—whether they were toddlers I'd never see again or baseball stars vomiting in the bushes and crying about the mother who never loved them.

By senior year, a bunch of us would gather on Friday nights in a parking lot behind an apartment complex. Not just drama kids, but drill team dancers, band nerds, jocks, Bible bangers. We'd all gone to the devil's side now.

And the more I drank with them, the more I realized my

mother was right. We really were all the same. We'd all struggled, we'd all hurt. And nothing made me feel connected to the kids I once hated like sharing a beer or three. Alcohol is a loneliness drug. It has many powers, but to a teenager like me, none was more enticing. No one had to be an outsider anymore. Everyone liked everyone else when we were drinking, as though some fresh powder of belonging had been crop-dusted over the Commons.

I WENT TO college in Austin. All that big talk of getting the hell out of town, and I only made it 180 miles south on the highway.

For years, people assured me I was a "college girl," which is what adults tell smart girls who fail to be popular. I assumed the transition would be a cinch. But I lived in a sprawling dorm that was more like a prison. I stood at social events in my halter top and dangly earrings, looking like the preppies my fashionably rumpled classmates abhorred. "You're so *Dallas*," one guy told me, which I understood to be an insult. (My first lesson in college: Hate the place you came from.) Other kids wore torn jeans and baby-doll dresses and clunky Doc Martens. I'd spent four years in a back bend trying to fit in at an upscale high school. Now I was going to have to contort myself all over again.

The first month was a terrible solitude. I took walks around the track behind the dorm, trying to lose those last stubborn pounds. I woke up early to apply makeup before my 8 am German class. Every once in a while, I ran into my high school boyfriend, Miles, on campus. We'd broken up over the summer, but we'd both come to the same state university, which was a bit like attempting a dramatic exit from a room only to discover the door was locked. Some nights, I lay in my prison bed and listened to U2's "One" on my CD Discman—the same anguished song, over and over, because I liked to curl up inside my own suffering and stay for a while.

Luckily, I found Anna. She was my peer advisor, which meant it was in her actual job description to help me out of my misery. She was a year older, with tastes I recognized as sophisticated. She drank her coffee black. She read Sylvia Plath, required reading for college girls dabbling in darkness, and Anne Sexton, whose very name told me something crazy was going on there. I'd only worshipped male artists—not on purpose so much as default—but Anna was drawn to the women. The secret diary writers, the singer-songwriters who strummed out their heartbreak, the girls splintered by madness. She had an Edward Hopper painting called *The Automat* over her desk. Nothing was happening in the picture, but it pulled me in anyway: a woman by herself, eyes cast downward, in an empty restaurant at night. Meanwhile, I decorated my work space with snapshots from high school dances where I clutched a gaggle of friends smiling on cue. I don't think I'd ever realized how beautiful a woman alone could be.

Anna and I became close that fall while acting in a shoestring production of a Chris Durang play. (Neither of us studied drama in college, but our small liberal arts program was the type where kids put on shows for the hell of it.) We were walking home from a rehearsal when she asked if I wanted to smoke a cigarette in her friend's dorm. He was out of town for a few days, and we would have the whole 100-square-foot cell block to ourselves.

It was one of those nights when a casual conversation unfolds into a fateful conversation. One Marlboro Light turned into a whole pack. Two Diet Cokes turned into half a dozen and a cheese pizza. We laid out the sad tales of our past like a Shinsu knife collection. *And here on the right, please admire my awkward first sexual experiences. Oooh, and have I shown you my bitter regret?*

I talked a lot about Miles that night. He and I had an ideal high school romance (except for the part where I cheated on him). He was hilarious and tender, a John Cusack of my very own (except for the part where he broke up with me after I cheated on him). The mature side of my brain knew our relationship had found its natural end. But my girlish heart kept getting tugged back to him. Sometimes I saw him on campus, walking with a girl who wore combat boots and a motorcycle jacket, and I felt like I'd been cattle-prodded. *Who the hell is she?*

To make it more confounding, Miles wasn't the same person I once dated. College was like a phone-booth identity swap for him. He wore a rainbow knit beret now and grew his cute floppy bangs into long spiraling curls. His goatee came to a point, like a billy goat, or Satan. As if he were daring me not to love him anymore.

But I couldn't stop, I explained to Anna as she nudged a box of Kleenex my way. I couldn't let go of him, even though I didn't know him anymore. College girls weren't supposed to be like this. We were supposed to be cool. Unencumbered. Free. Instead, I'd become one of Those Girls—the ones who drag their high school romance across the first year of college like a teddy bear on the ground. As for the actual teddy bear Miles gave me, I still slept with it every night.

Anna didn't have a boyfriend in high school. She was the valedictorian, and her closest companions had been novels. She knew books the way I knew pop songs, and listening to her sometimes made me wonder what I might have learned if I'd actually tried in my classes.

Anna was also proof that not all teenagers drink. She told me about this time when she was 18. She had gone to a bar and seen two cute boys. She wanted to impress them, so she picked up someone else's beer can and gestured with it while she spoke. When the cops walked in, the guys darted for the exit, while Anna got her first ticket. Anyone who got caught by the police said the same thing. "But, Officer, it's not mine." And Anna might have been the first kid in history to be telling the truth.

We talked till dawn that night, and I was exhausted and exhilarated by the time I returned to my thin foam mattress. Sometimes I call this evening "the night Anna and I fell in love," and sometimes I call it "the first night of our lives together," but I can't call it "the night we chain-smoked and ate cheese pizza in Mark's dorm room," because that happened pretty often.

In the later years of college, she and I would drink wine on friends' porches and sit together at picnic tables messy with tortilla chips and margarita spills. Anna knew how to knock back drinks by then. But in the first year we spent together, our adventures were limited to a 14-story dorm. We made each other mix tapes. We wrote each other handwritten letters and dropped them in the post office slot, even though we lived 150 feet apart, because we both understood the rush of getting mail. And through our long and loping conversations, I began to discover Anna had an industrial-grade memory. She could recall the most mundane details of my past. The make and model of Miles's car. The names of my cousins. It goosed me each time, like she'd been reading my journal.

Back in high school, an impeccable memory had been *my* superpower. I had archives of useless knowledge: the number of singles released from *Thriller* (seven), the actor who played the villain in *The Karate Kid* (Billy Zabka). Friends used to rely on me to fill in the backstory about our shared past. This was before the Internet, when the very act of remembering could make me feel like a whiz kid bound for a *Jeopardy!* championship. *What was the name of our freshman-year health teacher again? Where was that concert we went to in ninth grade?*

And I would think, "How can people forget their own lives?"

But college introduced me to people like Anna, whose memories surpassed my own. And I was dazzled by this, but I was also a bit intimidated, like a star high school athlete who's joined the pros.

"How can you remember that?" I would ask her, dumbstruck.

And she would arch her left eyebrow, her favorite pose of feminine mystery, and let the question dangle.

I tried to match her. I squirreled away biographical driftwood to lob into our conversations for a future surprise. Bam! Bet you didn't think I knew the name of your old coworker at the IHOP. Boom! Didn't realize I knew who sat beside you in philosophy, did you? My shelves were filled with books I could not finish and textbooks I never cracked. But I was always cramming for the test about Anna's past. I paid lavish attention to every word she spoke. Until then, it had not occurred to me what an act of love this was: to remember another person's life.

⁓

I STARTED SPENDING more time with Miles in our spring semester. We were trying to be "friends," which is another way of saying I wanted to get back together, and he wanted to sleep with me. It was working out pretty well.

I ditched the dining hall for evenings in his dorm watching old *Star Trek* episodes with the guys from down the hall. I was bored by *Star Trek*, but I liked being the only girl surrounded by that boy stink. They passed around a bong, letting their minds expand, while I settled in a beanbag and drank my Carlo Rossi wine (one jug for $5.99).

Miles loved pot. It fixed him, the way booze fixed me. I

smoked with him twice, and both times I forgot simple words. Like "chair" and "desk." Pot did the opposite of what I wanted from an illicit substance. It shut me down, turned me paranoid. I'd also read pot affected your long-term memory, and I worried what might happen to Miles if he continued to use. Back in high school, he was quick-witted, sharp, but now his voice could acquire such a thick syrup. Heeeeey, duuuuude.

I was scared of drugs. I never told Miles this, because I wanted to be close again, but I thought drugs were dirty and wrong and destructive. People often complain the "Just Say No to Drugs" campaign of the '80s was ineffective, but it worked on one person. I was afraid to touch any of that shit. *A line of cocaine made you drop dead. Heroin was a gun in your mouth.* As I sat there watching Miles load a pipe or tap out a flaky trail along a piece of thin and crinkly rolling paper, all I could think was: *Why can't you drink like normal people?*

But I kept hanging around him. I loved him—at least, I kept saying I did. And I knew if I stayed in his orbit long enough, his better judgment would drift out the window with his pot smoke and there was a good chance we'd end up in his bottom bunk once more.

"What does this mean?" I asked one morning, head on his chest.

He stared at the wooden plank above us. "It means we just slept together."

I didn't get it. I kept expecting him to revert to the role of high school boyfriend, snuggling in a booth built for two. But he was a college boy now, who wanted to live with all his doors and windows open. A few weeks later, I cleaned up his dorm room. Like a fucking den mother. I soaked the bowls crusted with cereal. Rinsed off and recycled the crumpled beer cans crawling with ants. I found two empty condom wrappers underneath his pillow, one more than we'd ever used, and I told myself: *Surely someone else borrowed his bed.* Nights got wild in his dorm, so it was possible. *Maybe a condom fell down from his roommate's bunk.* What an idiot. But a person can invent any stupid story to keep herself from uncomfortable truths.

A few nights later, I was hanging out in Miles's dorm room, but this time I wasn't the only girl. A pretty redhead shared her ideas about string theory. The girl with the combat boots and the motorcycle jacket dropped by. She was from Venezuela. And she said it with an accent—*Ven-ezz-waaay-luh*—like she was rubbing it in.

I took long slugs from my jug wine. I didn't care anymore. I was tired of counting calories, measuring each glass for its plea-sure, trying to lose five pounds so I could win back the boy who refused to be won. I drank cup after cup as I sat on the lower bunk and retreated into myself so far I could almost see us from space.

I could see that Miles and I would not get back together, and this was a good thing. I could see I was not the only girl for him. In fact, his life would be rich with women—smart, interesting women who might actually like *Star Trek*. These women would not apply mascara each morning, might not even shave their armpits, but he would dig that about them, the way he dug the girl from Venezuela, who wasn't even thin. She was full-bodied and foulmouthed, but he liked her because she was original and comfortable being something other than conventionally beauti-ful. Because she would suck a bong with him in rooms that were wisely unlit, while I stood in front of a magnifying mirror, add-ing sparkle shimmer to my eyes.

I left the room without saying good-bye. By the time I got back to my dorm, the wine had taken charge. I fell into the bushes outside the front entrance and spent a while digging around, trying to find the front door.

My last sustained memory is Anna, floating like an angel in a Cure T-shirt down the bright hallway. She held my hair as I threw up into her small sink, the one that kept moving. She changed me into a baggy T-shirt like she was putting a onesie on a limp baby.

Thank you, Anna. I'm so sorry, Anna. I love you, Anna.

"It's OK," she said with a gentle shush. "You're OK."

Over the years, I would become reliant on friends for the most basic information. How did we get home last night? Do you have any idea what happened to my jeans? Why is there a corn dog in my bed? After a while, I had to get more subtle—dig but not look like I was digging. "I had so much fun last night. What was the name of that bar again?" People repeated my antics back to me, and if I stayed still and laughed in the right spots, I could often complete the field report on my own behavior.

I have a picture of myself from that night. Taken after I blacked out. I'm sitting on the bed, my eyes so narrowed they nearly disappear when I smile. I don't know exactly why Anna took the photo. We were always documenting our lives back then, complimenting ourselves on how well we were living them. But this photo wasn't going to be tacked up in my work space. She later told me that after she snapped it, I began crying harder than she'd ever seen me cry. I became unreachable. A void in me had opened, and she had no idea how to fix me. I kept saying the same thing, over and over. *No one will ever love me. No one will ever love me.*

When Anna told me what happened, I was shaken. And I wasn't sure which worried me more: that I had blacked out again, or that when the deepest and truest part of me was cracked open, the only thing that poured out was need.

THREE

DRESSING IN MEN'S CLOTHES

I started wearing my dad's clothes in the fall of my sophomore year. I had raided his closet over the summer, plucking out a gray flannel shirt and a pair of Lee jeans, flecked with paint.

"Can I have this?" I asked.

And my father, confused. "What are you going to do with it?"

It must have been strange, to find his pint-size daughter rummaging through his battered old work clothes. But in the fall of 1993, the accidental lumberjack look was a uniform. I liked the drape of that flannel and how those jeans slid down my hips. I had to keep yanking them up, like a tiny girl in a giant's clothes.

I wore two of my dad's undershirts as well, which were thin and nearly transparent from multiple washings, so they had this luxurious softness. I liked that you could see straight through to my bra, which makes no sense, given the insecurity about my body that had dogged me since adolescence. But the shirt points to some essential conflict. A desire to flaunt and be masked at once. The undershirt was like a side door to exhibitionism. I had to be careful not to look too deliberate. That was the worst sin of all: trying too hard.

Sometimes I wore those undershirts inside out. I have no idea why I did this, except that it seemed daring to show a disregard for propriety.

"Your shirt's on inside out," a guy told me at a party.

"Your life's on inside out," I snapped back.

And he smiled. "You're right."

I had a crush on that guy. Mateo. He had a poof of curly hair like John Turturro in *Barton Fink*, and he was gruff and unsmiling like so many 19-year-olds. But if you nudged him right, he could be adorable and silly. I have a picture of him sitting in my apartment wearing my silky Victoria's Secret bra over his T-shirt and another of him paging through an old *Teen Beat* magazine with mock excitement.

My off-campus apartment was the party hub that year. The place was named the Casbah, so we were almost contractually obligated to rock it. My drink was Keystone Light. You could buy two six-packs of tall boys for five bucks at the Fiesta Mart—the equivalent of 16 beers for the price of a Wendy's value meal, which turned Keystone into the unofficial sponsor of our ragers.

That's what we called our parties: "ragers." A word associated with anger and weather systems, which is appropriate given the state of our living room the next day. Halogen lamp kicked over, beer bottle floating in the fish tank. *What the hell raged through here last night? Oh, yes. It was us. We raged.*

It was during one of these ragers at my apartment that Mateo and I had sex. At the time, we were in a play together, and we would sit in the dressing room before and during the show, knees brushing thighs. The flirtation had been building for weeks, but I needed some inciting incident. A match thrown on our diesel fuel. We were outside on the walkway of my crumbling cinder-block complex. I was chain-smoking, one cigarette lit on the tail end of another. And I said to him, with the confidence of six beers, "I bet you won't kiss me right now."

He was leaning against the wall. His forehead rippled as he looked up, all squint and slouch. He looked at the parking lot, at the dozens of people around us. He looked everywhere but at me. Then he said, "I don't think you're going to win that bet."

The idea of coming on to men was new. In high school, this would never have occurred to me. I had waited for Miles to kiss me, for months that felt like years. My coquettish signaling: sit next to him in class, play with my hair, cross my legs so they looked thinner. I read the tea leaves of his every gesture. *He called me last night. What does it meeaaaan?* This was how I understood seduction. Keep inviting the guy closer, but sit still until he pounces.

College flipped that script. The new imperative: If you want a guy, go after him. What's stopping you? We didn't use words like "feminism"—a fussy term for earlier generations, like "consciousness-raising" or the ERA—but it was understood that we ran with the boys. Argue with them. Challenge their ideas about sex and Ernest Hemingway, because they'd been holding the megaphone for too long, and we needed to wrest it from their grip. I even wore cologne. Calvin Klein's Obsession for Men. And slathering my neck in that rich, oaky musk gave me a kinky thrill, like I'd been rubbing up against some low-rent Johnny Depp.

But my lessons in women and power did not extend to the classroom. I was not a hand raiser of any kind. I took a C in my

Literature After the Holocaust seminar, because I couldn't force myself to open my mouth, despite participation being 25 percent of the grade. I ran into the professor on campus one day. She had dreads and a wry smile. I didn't even know they made professors this cool. We chatted for a bit, and she said, "I don't get it. Why didn't you ever talk in class?" And I blushed and said, "I'm shy," and she said, "Well, you shouldn't be."

No, I shouldn't be. I wasn't *meant* to be. And on the balcony of my apartment, I was not. Under cover of night and Keystone tall boys, I was full of righteous fire and brimstone. How I loved the taste of conviction in my mouth.

That is bullshit. You're wrong. Prove it.

I was done sucking up to men. Fluffing their egos. Folding their tightie whities. I was going to smash my bottles against the wall, and someone could clean up after me, goddammit. I stopped leaning over makeup mirrors and blow-drying my hair. I wore clothes that stank of hamper and Marlboro Lights, and it seemed to me that men got off on this new uncorseted persona. That's what they said: We like strong women. That's what they said: Be yourself. So, death to the girl of the nervous fidgets, behold the woman with a beer in her hand and one endless cigarette. No more hearts doodled in spiral notebooks. No more falling in love with every boy who looks your way in biology class. But falling into bed—now, this was another topic entirely.

That's what Mateo and I did that night. We slinked off into my bedroom while the party rambled on, and we ripped off each other's clothes in a blind, snarling rage. For so long, I wondered how it would feel to sleep with someone other than Miles. To run the tip of my nose along the powdery skin of his stomach, soft as a puppy's belly, and into the feral thicket of short, wiry hair leading down below. But I couldn't tell you what sex with

Mateo was like, because all I had the next day was a flash of a memory, five seconds of a frame: me, on top of him, my hands digging into his chest and my hair swishing around madly. I am told that I screamed. The kind of excitement that travels through flimsy apartment walls.

"I guess I don't need to ask if you enjoyed yourself," my roommate Tara said the next day over coffee.

But that seemed like a very good question. Honestly, I had no idea.

⌒

I LIKED THE idea of being "experienced." I was 16 when Miles and I had sex. I saw no explosion of glitter, no doves released into the air. Actually, it felt more like a bowling ball being shoved up my vagina (but a very sweet and loving bowling ball). I adored Miles. But our sex drives were set at different volumes. Mine was the medium hum of a transistor radio. His went to 11.

This is how teenage boys are, right? They'll hump anything. Hump the furniture. Hump the floorboards. Their dicks are like divining rods forever finding gold inside someone else's pants. And me? I was a cuddle bunny. I liked soft stroking and delicate kisses, and those nights could be a little heavy on the saliva and the grabbing for me.

I wasn't a prude or anything. That was a slur in high school. *Don't be a prude.* Guys would joke about girls so frigid their knees were sewn together and their tongues sat in their mouths like lazy slugs when you kissed them. I wasn't going to be that way. My tongue had a graceful twirl. My knees opened without a creak. My bra fell to the floor with a swoosh. I would pull a man in close, let him glide all over me, and my body parts went electric in his mouth. But then.

Then what?

I'm not going to say I faked orgasms. That sounds intentional. As if I knew what an orgasm felt like, and I purposefully pretended to be having one. It was more like: Orgasms happen when you're with men. You're with a man now. Are you having an orgasm? Probably so! I leaned in to those swells of pleasure with loud gasps and moans as if, by moving my arms and legs frantically enough, I might somehow learn to surf.

"Did you come?" Miles would ask, looking at me with those eager blue eyes.

And I would smile. "Yes." It was wish fulfillment, performance anxiety, and sexual ignorance wrapped up into one.

I wanted to be good in bed. Who doesn't want this? Are there women out there, hoping to be *bad* in bed? And I understood from NC-17 movies starring Mickey Rourke that being good in bed was a matter of arched backs and open mouths and frantic, animal fucking that ended in a double-orgasm thunderclap. It wasn't the hardest posture to imitate. Suck in your stomach, find the proper lighting, go nuts.

Being actually good in bed requires an openness, a comfort in your own body I simply did not have. The girl who once shaved off her pubic hair before sleepovers was not going to surrender to a man's touch so easily. I was wrapped up in "Do Not Cross" tape. I had moles on my back I never wanted Miles to see. I had bumpy skin on my upper arms (the name for this condition is folliculitis, an erotic term if ever there was one), and I would brush away Miles's hands while we were making out.

The problem—one of the many problems—is that I had very little knowledge of my own body and what might be pleasing to me, which made it impossible to give instructions to anyone else. It's like my vagina was someone else's playground. I'd never masturbated, and I don't know if that's because I was afraid, or ashamed, or simply uninterested. I guess I thought masturbation was for sad old divorcees who couldn't find anyone to finger-bang them. I was 25 when I finally bought a vibrator. The first time I came, the sensation was unmistakable. Like a long, ecstatic sneeze. And afterward, I felt so stupid. Wait a minute, *this* is an orgasm? Jesus Christ, no wonder everyone makes such a fuss about it.

But in college, what I knew best about my body was which parts other people liked. My boobs were like tractor beams on my chest, and I enjoyed being the source of awe and admiration, so I liked to flash my brights once in a while. Plus, I liked that my rack moved attention away from my thighs and my ass. My genetic curse: short, Irish, potato-picking peasant thighs. Not the long, elegant gams of those girls in jean cutoffs, one pencil leg over the other. My skirts came to the knee.

And I kept my giant flannel shirt tied around my small waist, so that it covered my lower half. A casual kind of camouflage. *It's a little hot in here, I think I'll just completely block your view of my ass.*

Alcohol helped. Oh my God, it helped. Behind my fortress of empty beer cans, I was safe from fear and judgment. Alcohol loosened my hips, and pried open my fists, and after years of anxious hem-tugging, the freedom was incredible. It felt good to pee in alleyways, letting my bare feet sit there in the splash. It felt good to face-plant in a patch of grass or on the plush gray carpet of our apartment. It felt good to jump up on the couch and whip the flannel shirt from around my waist and lasso it over my head.

Booze gave me permission to do and be whatever I wanted.

So much of my life had been an endless loop of: "Where do you want to go to dinner?" / "I don't know, where do *you* want to go to dinner?" But if I poured some of that gasoline in my tank, I was all mouth. *I want Taco Bell* now. *I want cigarettes* now. *I want Mateo* now. And the crazy thing about finally asking for what you wanted is that sometimes—oftentimes—you got it.

Did I think Mateo and I were going to get serious? Oh, please. I knew better than that. Which is to say: Yes, I wanted that, but I kept my teenage longing in check. I knew we weren't "dating," whatever that meant (a word from an earlier era, like "going steady" or "getting pinned"). We didn't even have the phrase "hooking up" then. It was just, you know, something. Mateo and I had *something*. Until it was nothing again.

The night after we had sex, Mateo showed up at my door. I was wearing striped flannel pajamas that swallowed me. Hangover clothes, a wearable blanket. I sat cross-legged on the couch as Mateo paced in front of the fish tank. He kept tugging on his poof of curly hair. He needed to say something, and he wasn't sure how to say it, but it needed to be said. OK, here it is: There was this other girl. A girl we both knew. A Winona Ryder type, with Bambi eyes and Converse sneakers. He and the other girl might be kinda-sorta seeing each other at the moment. And he wanted me to know that I was so great, and last night was so great, but the thing is. The problem is.

"I get it," I told him. "I totally understand."

"You do?" And he looked so grateful, and I was so happy to see him so happy. The easy extension of my hand at this moment punctured ten kinds of awkwardness between us, and I could feel the old rapport of the dressing room again. Everything was cool.

After he left, I called Anna, and I burst into tears.

I STARTED HANGING out with a guy named Dave. He was one of the many male friends I never slept with, and I couldn't tell if this was a tribute to our closeness or evidence of my supreme unfuckability. I loved being close to men and counseling them through their ill-advised one-night stands and teetering romances, but part of me wondered: *Why not me? Am I just not hot enough for you to imperil our amazing friendship?*

Dave and I liked to get drunk together and make each other laugh. Our nights were a game of comedic one-upmanship. How far can we push this moment? What never-before-seen trick can I invent? I was using a lot of moves from *Showgirls*, a terrible film about a dancer who becomes a stripper (or something). The movie was my favorite, because the dialogue was criminally heinous. Oh, the cheap high of youthful superiority: so much more fun to kick over sand castles than to build your own.

One night Dave and I were walking across the near-empty gardens of an Oktoberfest. I was drunk. (Of course I was drunk. I was always, always drunk.) A 70-year-old man in lederhosen approached us, bent like a candy cane, and I lifted up my shirt and flashed my bra. No warning, no prompting. Just: So wrong.

Dave almost fell to the cement he was laughing so hard. I got so high capsizing him this way. Because if I couldn't be the girl he loved—that would be my roommate, Tara—then I needed to be the girl who brought him to his knees.

Tara was a sweet roommate. She sang daffy little nonsense songs while she cooked eggs and bacon for Dave and me on a hungover Sunday. She decorated the apartment with sunflowers and flea-market knickknacks. She opened the curtains, and Dave and I hissed like vampires, but Tara knew the light would lift our moods. That's how I thought of her—as sunshine that spilled onto darkness. Nevertheless, one morning, she sat me down and gave me one of Those Talks. "You kept calling me a bitch last night," she said, and I thought: *No way. You're such a sweetheart.*

There was only one explanation for my behavior. It was the bourbon's fault.

Dave had turned us on to bourbon. Jim Beam. Maker's Mark. Evan Williams. He walked around our ragers with a tumbler, drinking his Manhattan. He was into that masculine romance: fast cars and cowboy boots and the throb of a blues song so old you could still hear the crackle in the recording. He referred to bourbon as a "real drink," which pissed me off so much I had to join him.

I had never cared much for liquor. To be honest, I was afraid of it. I liked the butterfly kisses of a light lager, which whisked me off into a carefully modulated oblivion, and bourbon was like being bent over a couch 20 minutes into your date. But Tara started drinking bourbon, and so obviously I had to follow.

My group made fun of girls who couldn't hold their booze. Girls who threw up after two drinks. Girls who needed to spike their cocktails with fruit and candy, turning their alcohol into birthday cake. I prided myself on a hearty constitution. So I sauntered up to those amber bottles, and I learned to swallow their violence. Do that enough, and you will reorient your whole pleasure system. Butterfly kisses become boring. You crave blood. *Hit me, motherfucker. Hit me harder this time.*

We were on a road trip to Dallas for the Texas-OU football game when I went off the rails. I never liked football. I hated the rah-rah gridiron nonsense that defined my alma mater and my home state. But Tara and Dave didn't share my grump. They had

insignia clothes and koozies and all that shit. One Friday afternoon, they loaded into a friend's Ford Explorer, and I had little
choice but to go with them. The only fate worse than football
was being left behind.

Dave was sitting in the passenger seat, controlling the flow
of music and booze. He mixed Jim Beam and Coke into plastic
cups big enough to swim in.

"Don't drink this too fast," he told me, because Dave was like
that. A protector. He'd been a lifeguard in high school, and he
still surveyed every party for anyone in danger of drowning.

"I won't. I promise," I said, which was not true. I couldn't help
drinking fast, because that's how I drank. I was a natural-born
guzzler. I was already on my second giant cup when we stopped
at a gas station 45 minutes outside Austin, and when I stood up,
all the booze whooshed through my system. I was like one of
those poker players in a Western who gets up from the table and
then keels over. The last thing I remember is standing outside
the bathroom unable to light a cigarette and some helpful person pointing out that it was in my mouth backward.

The next four hours are gone. Flushed down the toilet. My
parents were out of town that weekend, thank God, since I woke
up in their house in Dallas, snuggled up in my childhood bed,
naked and shivering, with a poster of James Dean pulled off the
wall and covering me like a blanket. Something had gone badly
wrong.

Tara was the one who told me. She called the next day, and
she had a frost in her voice. "People are a little upset right now,"
she said, and I twirled the phone cord tightly around my index
finger, watching the tip turn red, then white. It was no small
feat, turning a group of binge-drinking tailgaters against you.

The story I could not remember would be told many times.

We had just reached the city limits of Dallas when I decided to moon people. The mooning scene is a staple of '80s sex comedies—the *Animal House* genre of films about prep school boys busting out of their conformist youth. And I'd like to think I was paying tribute to those classic films. Except I botched a few key details. One is that I was surrounded not by like-minded brothers but irritated college friends who were not nearly so cross-eyed with drink. Another is that the mooning scene in those films took place while the boys were hurtling along a highway at night, and mine took place in five o'clock traffic. Yes, I mooned cars in a bumper-to-bumper snarl down the interstate, which is a little bit like mooning someone and then being stuck in a grocery line with them for the next ten minutes. *Hey, how's it going? Yeah, sorry our friend is mooning you right now, she's really drunk. Excited about the game?*

But the third and most critical difference is that I was a girl. And for a girl, there is good nudity (boob shaking, leg spreading) and then there is bad nudity (sitting on a toilet, plucking hairs from your nipple). Pressing your wide white ass up to the window of a vehicle in broad daylight is *definitely* in the column of bad nudity.

The next week was a humiliation buffet. There are times when you want to die. And then there are times when one death is simply not enough. You need to borrow other people's lives and end them, too. All death, everywhere, seems like the only way to extinguish your agony, and while this story would become funny in time, I can assure you that in the moment, I believed I only had two options. Destroy everyone in the car. Or never drink bourbon again.

I quit brown liquor that day. *Never again*, I told myself. Not every catastrophe can be solved so easily, but this one only took a simple snip, and I was allowed to stay on the party train for many more years. Everyone forgave me, which is the grace of college. We all had dirty pictures on each other.

But still, I wondered: Why was I like this? College is a time to discover yourself—and alcohol is the Great Revealer—but I was more corkscrewed than ever. What did it mean that I hid when I was sober, and I stripped off all my clothes when I was blind drunk? What did it mean that I adored my roommate, but I lashed out at her after seven drinks? What did it mean that I didn't love Dave (or maybe I did), but I would slay dragons to win his approval? I needed to expose the deeper meaning here. I needed to workshop this fucker.

I FINALLY GOT a boyfriend near the end of college. And the weirdest part was: He didn't drink. This was unbelievable to me. He used to drink, but he no longer drank. *By choice.* We met at a party, where he was dressed like he'd stepped out of a 1960s gin ad. He pulled out a gold Zippo and ignited it with a magnificent scratch, lighting two Camels at once before handing me one. Like he was Frank Sinatra.

Two weeks later, we took a road trip and slept in a tent under the stars somewhere in northern New Mexico. I hadn't done such a thing since I was a girl. It had never occurred to me camping was something you'd do on purpose. As I marveled at the red-rock canyons of the Southwest, I thought: Where did this beauty come from? Has it been here all along?

Patrick was a professional cook. He would come home from work after midnight, his clothes smelling of wood-burning ovens, his fingertips marked by burns in the shape of purple crescent moons. His friends were cooks and fellow hedonists, who drank fine wine and had serious thoughts on plating, and for a while, I wondered what he saw in me. But unlocking the world for someone else can bring such pleasure. He gave me Tom Waits, Pacific oysters, and a knowledge of the shiver that might run through me when a man traced one index finger across the tender spots of my back.

We hung out in pool halls. I liked billiards—such a dude's sport, such a hustler's game—but before I met Patrick, I had no idea how to play, and so I simply imitated power. My shots were all random thrust, because I enjoyed the clink of the balls scattering around the table like buckshot. But Patrick showed me finesse. He knew how to move.

"Slow down," he teased me, positioning himself behind me, and he taught me how to sink my body in order to level my gaze, how to drag the cue stick across the cradle of my fingers, slow and gentle, like I was drawing back a bow. He taught me how to torque a ball with English, wrap the cue behind my back if I needed to, and tap the ball with just the right amount of force so that it slid across the green felt and dropped into the trickiest corner pocket with a quiet *thump*. "Only use force when you need it," he would say, cigarette dangling from his lips, and then he'd hammer a shot right into the corner. Bam. Sunk.

I was not wearing my father's jeans anymore. I was wearing tight pencil skirts and black dresses that hugged my curves. I dyed my hair auburn. Patrick was with me when I took my first legal drink. He brought me to a cigar bar called Speakeasy, a trendy Prohibition throwback that had recently opened in the burned-out warehouse district. I ordered a vodka martini. "You'll like it dirty," Patrick told me, and once again, he was right.

But booze became an argument between us. The more I drank, the more I wanted him, and the less he wanted me.

"You're lit again," he would say, pushing me away as I barreled toward him, having finally drunk myself into a place of unbridled wanting. Maybe it sounds odd that a recovering alcoholic would take up with a problem drinker, but we were familiar to each other. We beckoned from forbidden sides. In me he saw his past decadence. In him I saw my future hope. And it worked. For a while.

Six months after we started dating, Patrick turned to me one night and told me he didn't love me anymore. The best way to explain how I took this news is to tell you I didn't date anyone for seven years.

But I beat a lot of men at pool. I watched out of the corner of my eye as their nostrils flared, and they stamped their cue on the ground, and their eyes tracked me around that table. Were they gonna get beaten by a girl? At least two of my one-night stands began this way. Most of the others? It's hard to remember how they began.

FOUR

DRINK MORE AT WORK

I wanted to be a writer since I was a little girl. Actually, I wanted to be a writer-actress-director (and, for a brief and confusing time, a Dallas Cowboys cheerleader-writer-actress-director). But I made up my own worlds; I didn't report on real ones. I never even considered journalism until my roommate Tara became the head of our college daily and invited me to contribute. I walked down into a dingy basement where pale chain-smokers argued about school vouchers. A sign hung at the entrance. *Welcome to the* Daily Texan—*where GPAs go to die.*

I found a home in the entertainment section, which allowed me to cover any theater production in town, while boys in ratty concert T-shirts grappled for the latest Pavement album. It hadn't occurred to me I could write a story *today,* and it could show up on your kitchen table *tomorrow.* What a rush. There are wonderful reasons to become a journalist. To champion the underdog. To be professionally curious. Me? I just wanted to get free stuff and see my name in print.

And I was charmed by the companionship of the newsroom.

Writing had always been a solitary pursuit, but winding my way alongside those cubicles full of keyboard clatter felt like being backstage before a show. I had stopped acting, in part because I'd grown uncomfortable with people looking at me. Journalism offered a new kind of exposure, like performing on a stage with the curtains closed.

At 23, I landed a gig at a beloved alt weekly called the *Austin Chronicle*, and I couldn't have been more ecstatic. A real-live salary. Something called "health benefits." I felt like I was standing on the first step of a staircase that stretched all the way to— why not?—the *New York Times*. Then again, the *Chronicle* was the kind of place a person wouldn't mind staying forever. Staffers wore flip-flops and arrived after 10 am. A group got stoned by the big tree each afternoon, and production halted at 5 for a volleyball game. Each morning, a woman appeared in the lobby to sell breakfast tacos for a dollar, one of a million reasons Austin was amazing: random people showing up out of nowhere to hand out hangover food.

My desk was in front of a brick wall that I decorated with a giant poster from the musical *Rent*. I'd bought the poster on my first trip to New York City, where I visited my brother, who was in grad school there. He'd taken me to a Broadway show, and I sat in those squeaky seats watching a vision of bohemia I hoped might one day be mine: documentarians with spiky gelled hair, drug addict musicians, lipstick lesbians in black catsuits.

A week after I started at the paper, a scruffy guy from production stopped in front of the poster, pointed to it, and shook his head. "Seriously?" he said, and moved on.

I didn't know *Rent* had become a punch line of '90s sincerity and manufactured edge. I didn't realize AIDS victims singing in five-part harmony about seasons of love could make some of my colleagues want to punch an old lady in the neck. But that day I learned my first lesson in pop-culture tyranny: Subjective tastes can be wrong.

That Saturday, when no one was around, I took down *Rent* and replaced it with *Blade Runner*, a film beloved by sci-fi nerds and cinephiles, although I wasn't certain why. I'd only seen it once, and fallen asleep.

The production guy passed my desk again on Monday. "Now we're talking," he said, giving me the thumbs-up, and moved on.

I'd always considered myself fluent in pop culture, but the *Chronicle* was a crash course in acceptable indie tastes. I kept a mental list of artists I needed to become familiar with, much like the vocab words I used to memorize in middle school to casually drop into conversation. Jim Jarmusch, François Truffaut, Albert Maysles. The Velvet Underground, Jeff Buckley, Sonic Youth. The spirit of an alt weekly, after all, was to be an alternative. Our mandate dictated that the most important stories lived outside the mainstream. And also: Top 40 sucked.

Every Thursday afternoon, the staff gathered in a cramped meeting room that looked more like a bomb shelter and lined up stories for the week. Debates were always breaking out, because those people could argue about anything: the most overrated grunge band, the notion of objective journalism, black beans or refried. I sat with my hands in my lap and hoped to God the conversation wouldn't drift my way. But when the meeting ended, and nobody had called on me, I'd feel weirdly crestfallen. All that anxious buildup for nothing.

I've always been mixed up about attention, enjoying its warmth but not its scrutiny. I swear I've spent half my life hiding behind a couch and the other half wondering why no one was paying attention to me.

On the weekends, coworkers and I started going to karaoke, which was the perfect end run around my self-doubt. I would sit in the audience, drinking beer after beer, filling myself up with enough "fuck it" to take the microphone. Karaoke was a direct line to the parts of our brains unburdened by aesthetics, the child who once found joy in a Journey song. No singer was bad, no taste was wrong—which was pretty much the inverse philosophy of the paper, but my coworkers still loved it. I guess even people who judge others for a living can secretly long for a world with no judgment.

At our holiday karaoke party, I blew out my vocal cords with an over-the-top version of "Total Eclipse of the Heart." I was in that sparkling state of inebriation where the chain comes off your inhibitions and your voice grows so bold.

The following Monday, our cranky editor-in-chief kicked off the staff meeting. "I have one thing to say about the holiday party." He turned toward me, and his eyes lit up. *"Sarah Fucking Hepola."*

You could've seen my glow from space. Before that, I wasn't even sure he knew my last name.

❧

GROWING UP, I saw journalism as a serious profession. I never anticipated how much damn fun it would be. Music festivals, interviews with celebrities, parties where Quentin Tarantino showed up. Dot-com money was pouring into our flophouse hamlet, and the city's growth made the paper fat with advertising. We got bonus checks and open-bar celebrations. Coming to the *Chronicle* a year after college was like leaving a five-year house party only to plunk down on the ripped couches of never-never land.

Swag. That was the name for the promotional items that

arrived with alarming abundance. T-shirts, tote bags, novelty toys. For a year, a beach ball with the words "There's Something About Mary" roamed through the hallway like a tumbleweed.

We got free movies and free CDs and free books. Complimentary bottles of Tito's Vodka lived in the kitchen. Shiner Bock popped up in the fridge (we paid for that). Each Wednesday night, we put the paper to bed—and those were the words we used, like the paper was our toddler—and I stayed late on the picnic table out back drinking with the proofreaders and the guys from production. We played games of "Who Would You Rather?" sorting the entire staff into people we would like to bang, careful to never mention each other.

I didn't write much at first. I ran the listings section and contributed third-string theater reviews with unnecessary adjectives. The young, hotshot music critic wrote with such wild metaphors, paragraphs like jazz riffs. I asked him once how he got so good, and he told me, "I did acid." But he also had what every writer needs: his own voice.

I did not. My writing was a kind of literary karaoke. I aped the formulas and phrasings of older critics whose work I admired. I sometimes borrowed friends' opinions for theater reviews, because I was certain theirs were more accurate than my own. I'd sit each week in the meeting, listening to the lineup of cover stories, wanting that spotlight so badly. But what did I have to say?

In college, I never read newspapers, which made it a tiny bit awkward to be working for one. What did people want from their news? The *Chronicle* offered two primary channels, criticism and reporting. But I had neither the deep knowledge nor the training for either. My colleagues slung their authority around the room, while I became afraid to botch any answer. Black or refried: Which *are* the superior beans?

As for my artistic tastes, I wasn't sure about them, either. We had entered the Age of Irony. Low culture was high culture, and the difference between loving something and hating it was razor thin. People like me disguised our true feelings in layers of detachment, endless pop-culture references, sarcasm. Because no one can break your heart if they don't know it.

I pulled down the *Blade Runner* poster and put up a picture of the Backstreet Boys, and I forced everyone on staff to vote on their favorite member.

"I don't fucking know," the cranky editor-in-chief said when I stopped him in the hallway. "The blond one, with the nice smile."

About nine months after coming to the paper, I got my first big assignment. I went undercover to high school prom. The mass shooting at Columbine had taken place a few months prior, leading to a glut of paranoid articles about "teens today," and my story was the kind of goofy, first-person escapade almost guaranteed to wind up on the cover.

There was one problem. I was so freaked out by the pressure I couldn't write a word. I spent hours staring at a blinking cursor, typing words only to erase them again. The night before the piece was due, desperate for any fix, I opened a bottle of wine. *Fuck it. Maybe this will help.*

Before then, I never drank while I was writing. I might have downed a few beers while I waited on page edits. But writing and drinking were two fundamentally opposing activities—like eating and swimming. Writing required hush and sharpness of vision. Drinking was roar and blur.

The wine turned down the volume on my own self-doubt, which is what a blocked writer is battling: the bullying voices in her head telling her each thought is unoriginal, each word too ordinary. Drug users talk about accessing a higher conscious-ness, a doorway to another dimension—but I just needed a giant fishhook to drag my inner critic out of the room.

That night, I drank myself into the writing zone. Words tum-bled from my fingers like they'd been waiting to get shaken loose. I couldn't believe how well it worked. After the story came out, staff members stopped me in the hall to quote their favorite lines.

So, of course, this became a common practice. A couple glasses to prime the pump. Sometimes, in the privacy of my funky little garage apartment, I would drink myself blind. I purposefully did this—drank myself to the place where I was clattering all over the keyboard with my eyes drooped to half-moons, free as Ray Charles over his piano, and you'd think this would result in reams of nonsense, and sometimes it did. Other times, I'd find myself reading over the words later and thinking: *Wow, this is pretty good. I didn't even know I thought that.* Those pages were full of typos and run-ons, but they had the hypnotic clickety-clak of a train barreling across the high plains. They had the last-call honesty of someone pulling the listener close. *We only have a few more minutes. Let me tell you everything.*

People sometimes ask me how someone can drink so much and still keep her job. But drinkers find the right job.

After drawing my name for Secret Santa, the editor-in-chief gave me a hat with beer holders on either side. "So you can drink more at work," he said.

❧

ON MY TWENTY-FIFTH birthday, I drove out to visit Anna. She had moved to San Francisco, where she wrote me long letters from a café near Golden Gate Park, and her voice had the lightness of a girl in constant hop-skip.

But I don't think I've ever felt as bitter and depressed about a birthday as I did at 25. This may sound strange, given how young that is, and given how great my job was, but 25-year-olds are experts at identifying what the world has not given them, and that birthday was like a monument to everything I hadn't achieved. No boyfriend. No book deal. Only the flimsiest kind of fame. "I saw your name in the paper," people said to me. Why did they think this was a compliment? *I saw your name.* Oh, thanks. Did you bother to read the next 2,000 words?

My friends had escaped to grown-up jobs in coastal cities, and I chided myself for lacking the gumption to follow. Anna was out in California seeking social justice through a series of impressive nonprofit law gigs. My old roommate Tara was a reporter in Washington, DC. My friend Lisa, hired at the *Chronicle* alongside me, had ventured to Manhattan and gotten a gig at the *New York Times.*

"You should move out here," she would tell me, on our phone dates, and I told her I couldn't afford it. The more accurate reason: I was scared.

My high school drama friend Stephanie wasn't. She had been living in New York for a few years and already become one of those rare creatures, a successful actress. She landed a role as an attorney in an NBC crime drama also starring '80s rapper Ice-T. *SVU*, it was called, though I liked to call it "SUV." She had made it in the big city, just like we said we would, and I watched her ascend in a gilded hot air balloon, as I stood on the ground and counted the ways life had failed me.

I was particularly burned up on the boyfriend issue. I thought having a byline in the *Austin Chronicle* would bring cute, artistic men to my doorstep, but it really only brought publicists. Years of Shiner Bock and cheese enchiladas had plumped me by at least 40 pounds, which I masked in loose V-necks and rayon skirts scraping the ground, but I also spied a double standard at play. Male staffers dressed like slobs, but they still found pretty girls to wipe their mouths and coo over their bands. Meanwhile, I was nothing but a cool sisterly type to them. Where were my flirty emails? My zippy office come-ons? How come nobody wanted to fuck *me* for my talent?

So I needed that road trip to California. Five days by myself through West Texas, New Mexico, across the orange Cream-sicle of the Nevada desert at sunset. In Las Vegas, I booked my room at the demented-circus hotel Hunter S. Thompson wrote about in *Fear and Loathing*. It pains me to admit I had never read this book. But I understood Thompson's work to be a locus of debauchery and creative nonfiction, the intersection where I planned to build my bungalow.

I slummed around the nickel arcades on the low-rent side of the Strip that night, and I won $200 at a machine that was clearly broken, so all you had to do was mash the same button over and over again, winning every time. A brunette in a French maid skirt brought me a check, but there were no flashing lights on the arcade. No coins clinking into my bucket. It's weird how you can hit the jackpot—and still feel a little robbed.

The sky was dark when I got to Anna's place, and she was standing on the corner when I pulled up, doing her jokey little happy dance in the beams of my headlights, biting her lower lip and swaying.

"What does a girl have to do to get a drink around here?" I asked, and we smiled like two people who have crossed great distances to find each other. But when she pulled my bags out of the car, something sank in her and never reappeared. Was she mad about how late it had gotten? Was she disappointed to see

I'd gained so much weight? Best friends have a spooky voodoo. We're like cats on airplanes, who can feel each dip in cabin pressure, and at that moment, Anna and I took a nosedive.

The way Anna tells it, she came to my car and saw a bunch of empty beer cans clattering around in the backseat. It was her epiphany moment. I'd been alone on that trip. I'd been immersed in solo adventure and the majesty of the outdoors, and yet I could not let go of my cheap silver crutches from 7-Eleven. The funny truth is that I drank less on that trip than I usually did. Even now there's a defiant part of me that wants to correct her observation. Like I was being punished not for my indulgence but for a commitment to recycling.

Anna knew other stories, though. Troubling episodes that had accumulated. On my visit to New York, I got so drunk I fell down a flight of stairs and ended up in the hospital with a concussion. One night in Austin, I went out to karaoke with friends, and I was so loaded I jumped onstage and wrestled the microphone from some poor guy in the middle of "Little Red Corvette." When I went to get a drink afterward, the bartender said, "I'm sorry, you've been cut off." Cut off? Why? For nailing that fucking Prince song?

There were stories about questionable men, and trips to Planned Parenthood the next morning, and a stubborn refusal to use condoms followed by a terrible guilt. And once I told Anna these secrets, I felt purged and hopeful. But I'd laid a heavy heap of jagged worry in her arms.

After I got back to Texas, Anna sent me another letter. Her voice did not have the hop-skip this time. I read it with a thunderstorm rolling in my belly, the words of rejection leaping out as if a yellow highlighter had been dragged across them: "worried about you." "can no longer watch." "please understand." She did not demand that I quit drinking, but she told me she couldn't be the safe place for my confessions anymore. It was a love letter, the hardest kind to write, but I did not see it that way. It felt like a bedroom door slammed in my face.

A YEAR LATER, I quit drinking. Not forever, but for 18 months, which felt like forever. And in that stretch of sobriety, much of my happiness came back to me. Weight dropped off my hips. My checking account grew heavy with unused beer money. I took off the hair shirt of my own entitlement and began reaching for the life I wanted. One day, I walked into the editor-in-chief's office, closed the door behind me, and told him I was moving to Ecuador.

The travel part of my story is one of the greatest times of my life. Scary, but thrilling: Ecuador, Peru, Bolivia. I read books half the day and spent the rest of the hours however I wanted.

But be careful when you finally get happy. Because you can become greedy for the one thing you don't have.

I missed drinking. This new world was grand, but I didn't feel complete without that foamy abandon. I thought about drinking all the time. If only I could drink again, then I could lose myself to this handsome stranger and not be hobbled by my own nagging insecurities. If only I could slurp down those *pisco* sours like the other students at the Spanish school, I could let foreign words spill out of my mouth like divine prophecy instead of being so scared to speak in Spanish that I ducked eye contact. I was 27 years old, and I had everything—except the delicious communion of two beers, maybe three. I wanted so badly to dip a toe in that river again. Dip a toe, or maybe fall in.

My fever grew stronger, and I began to itch for the drama of drinking. You know what I miss? A hangover. You know what I want? A night I regret. My shins covered in eggplant bruises, some unshaven backpacker at the book depot, his hands all over me.

Three months into my trip, Ecuador qualified for the World Cup for the first time in history, and I didn't give a rip about soccer, but I needed to celebrate. A party broke out in the square. I cracked open a 20-ounce beer, took a swig, and felt a loosening that traveled down to my toes. Two hours and two beers later, I was crazy-dancing to Shakira, the Spanish-language version, on the front patio of my lodge alone. Fuck judgment. Fuck discretion. *I was back.*

When I returned to the States, I struggled to explain to my friends why I had started drinking again. After all, not much time had passed since I explained to them why I quit. But I told them I was healthier now. I would be careful. My friends mostly nodded and tried to figure out which reaction would be supportive and which would be naive. "People come in and out of sobriety all the time," I said, and as we rambled into our late 20s, these were the bumpy roads we had to navigate: Marriages fail, lesbians start dating men again, dreams turn out to be the wrong dreams.

A few weeks later, I had another blackout. This time in front of 300 people.

I HAD BEEN hanging out with a trio of comedians, and their ability to extemporize dazzled me. Each time they unhinged their subconscious, hilarity fell out. When one of them asked me to perform at an event he was hosting, I wanted to be bold enough to join them. Take a chance. Risk failure. As Elliott Smith sang: *"Say yes."*

So I said yes, but to what? I had no improv skills and couldn't play an instrument. We settled on what we called a "Drunken Q&A." I would get buzzed, and audience members could ask me anything they wanted. Easy, right? I had no idea hundreds of people would show.

I also didn't expect the guy I'd been seeing in Dallas to come. Lindsay and I had been dabbling in a relationship for two weeks, long emails and after-hours phone calls, and I was wrestling with how serious we should be. I liked him, but did I like him enough? He surprised me that night—driving three hours to watch me perform in Austin, a grand gesture that made me nervous and spazzy. I was excited he wanted to be there but worried I couldn't match his enthusiasm, or the adoring way he looked at me, and the answer to this pinwheel of anxiety was to drink. A lot.

By the time the show started, I was stumbling across the open grassy area, stopping people who passed. "Have you met my new boyfriend?" I asked, one hand in his and another around a cup of wine. "He's *cuuuuuute*."

I made it to the stage soon after, and people asked their questions. But the only part I remember is telling a very disjointed story about Winnie-the-Pooh.

When I woke the next morning, I felt shattered. I'd spent the past two years on a path of evolution—but here I was, crawling back under the same old rock. Lindsay and I walked to a coffee shop, where a guy on the patio recognized me. "Hey, you're the drunk girl from last night," he said, and my stomach dipped. "You were hilarious!"

I've heard stories of pilots who fly planes in a blackout, or people operating complicated machinery. And somehow, in this empty state, I had stood on a stage, opened my subconscious, and hilarity fell out.

I turned to my new boyfriend, to gauge his response. He was beaming. "You're famous now," he said, and squeezed my hand.

I moved to Dallas to live with Lindsay and became the music critic at the *Dallas Observer*. Another stint on the good-times van. Club owners floated my tab, label owners bought me drinks. I was barely qualified for the job, and I faked my way through half my conversations, but the alcohol cushioned my mistakes. So did my boyfriend. Lindsay was a closet artist, who spent his evenings fiddling with song mixes and his days building databases. My new gig was an all-access pass to a world he'd only seen from a middle row. "I feel like the president's wife," he told me one night, after we spent the evening drinking with musicians. It didn't even occur to me that might be a bad thing.

My stories were gaining traction. I began writing in a persona that was like me, only drunker, more of a comedic mess. I made jokes about never listening to albums sent by aspiring bands, which was neither that funny nor that much of a joke. But people told me I was a riot. Maybe they liked being reminded we were all screwed up, that behind every smile lurked a disaster story. I began contributing to a scrappy online literary magazine called *The Morning News*. And in this tucked-away corner of the Internet, where I could pretend no one was watching, I began to write stories that sounded an awful lot like the real me.

People *were* watching, though. An editor at the *New York Times* sent me an email out of nowhere. She wondered if I'd like to contribute a piece sometime. They were looking for writers with voice.

LINDSAY AND I made a good pair. He cooked elaborate dinners—lamb souvlaki, Thai lemongrass soup—as I dangled my feet from the kitchen counter, sipping wine from balloon glasses that were like fishbowls on a stick. He liked taking care of me, although we both liked not taking care of ourselves. Our lives felt like a Wilco song: *The ashtray says you were up all night.* Our lives felt like an Old 97's song: *Will you sober up and let me down?* Those were the songs we listened to while chain-smoking out a window, songs assuring us if you're hurting and hungover, then you're doing it right.

On Saturdays, we would heal ourselves with a greasy Mexican breakfast. Eggs, cheese, chorizo. Sometimes we wondered aloud if ours was the right path. Weren't we supposed to be building something of meaning? We were 29 years old, the same age my mother was when she had me. Lindsay talked about his father, who had moved all the way from Australia and started his own business. What had *we* done?

But then we'd go to the bar and just repeat what we'd done the night before. The bartender poured my Harp as soon I walked in the door. *I had arrived.*

Lindsay and I drank together, and we drank a lot. But I was the one with the bruises and bumps. I had a habit of slipping off sidewalk curbs while we stood there at the end of the night.

"I don't get it," I told Anna, on one of our regular phone dates. "He drinks as much as I do."

"He's a foot taller than you!" she said.

I still confided in Anna, but with more line-editing now. I told her enough to maintain our closeness but not enough to cause worry. The troubled drinker's sleight of hand—dividing your confessions among close friends but never leaving any one person doused with too much truth.

Anna might not have been worried, but I was. Lindsay and I worked on paper, but I couldn't lose the nagging suspicion we were missing an essential spark. I wanted more, but I also thought maybe I was being unrealistic. What's the difference between a person who's unfulfilled and a person who's impossible to please?

Lindsay would leave for his office job at 8:30 in the morning, a full two hours before me, and I would walk him to the door and then climb back under the covers, feeling toxic and pointless again. His big orange tabby would hop up on the bed and curl up on my stomach, and I fucking loved that cat. Somehow, he made me feel forgiven.

I stopped calling the cat by his given name, a small act of rebellion that spoke to a much greater ambivalence. But the cat had been named for a status car, which was clearly a mistake, so I tried out new names, changing them each season until one finally took. Bubba. A proper name for a big orange tabby.

I guess we're stuck here, I'd say to Bubba as he curled up on my belly, although I knew it was only true for one of us. I *felt* stuck, though. Stuck in a life that was easy and indulgent and yet I could not get enough in my mouth.

If I had to guess the moment I knew Lindsay and I were in trouble, I would point to the night I stood up in the bathtub and he looked the other way. We used to slosh around after midnight in that claw-foot tub, naked and shameless, with our glasses chattering on the tile floor. But then one time I stood up, water rushing down my naked body, and he averted his eyes. He looked *embarrassed* for me. A betrayal contained in the tiniest flicker of a movement.

"Do you think I've gained weight?" I asked a few days later, with enough wine in my system to feel brave.

What could he possibly say: that I had not? He was an MBA who brought a protractor to every argument. He knew as well as I did my skirts didn't fit anymore. But I wanted him to tell me otherwise. To lie, to be oblivious, to convince me I looked beautiful anyway. "I think you've gained weight, yes. Ten, maybe fifteen pounds."

"*Ten*," I spit back. We both knew it was 20.

He never asked me to quit drinking. He asked me to drink like a normal person. To moderate. To maintain. And I began a series of shell games to get back to the way we were. Atkins Diet. South Beach Diet. If I could lose weight, he would look at me with those besotted eyes again. But the less I ate, the more I fell. I bashed my knee so badly I had to visit an orthopedic physician. I started enlisting Lindsay's help to keep me in check. Save me from myself.

"Don't let me have more than three drinks," I said as I got ready one night.

He put his hands on my shoulders. "If I see you with a fourth, I will karate-kick it out of your hands."

But after two beers, I didn't like our arrangement anymore. And I shot him a look like "If you take this fourth drink out of my hands, I will *cut* you."

I woke up to his back a lot of mornings. I started hanging out more with the guys from work. They still laughed when I knocked over my martini.

If I had to guess the moment *Lindsay* knew we were in trouble, I would point to the night I was so wasted I couldn't climb our back staircase, so he convinced me I was a kitty cat. I was in a blackout, and I crawled up the rickety steps on my hands and knees, meowing at the moon and trying to swish my nonexistent tail. But to Lindsay, this behavior was no longer cute, or funny, or endearing. It was pathetic.

I went to an alcohol therapist, my big display of I-mean-it-this-time. She had an office in the Dallas suburbs, in a home with too many cuckoo clocks.

"Men leave women who drink too much," she told me, as I tugged at the fraying ends on her couch. "He will leave you." I thought: *How is that fair? Women stay with men who drink too much all the time.* I thought: *But if I stop drinking, what would we do together?* I thought: *What the fuck does this woman know?*

A few months later, Lindsay turned to me after dinner in a shitty Greek restaurant, and he said, "I can't do this anymore." And I knew he did not mean the dinner in the shitty Greek restaurant.

I wasn't devastated; I was furious. In our time together, his stock only climbed. He was better-looking, dressed less like a business nerd and more like the East Dallas musicians I had introduced him to. Meanwhile, I felt like the fat drunk he was ditching on the side of the road. But underneath my wounded pride, I knew our split was right. I'd spent two and a half years unsure of my love for him and hating myself more and more. What I had required was unfair. I wanted him to love me enough for both of us.

I needed to change. I needed to turn my life into something I didn't need to drink to tolerate. The day after Lindsay broke up with me, I made a decision.

"I'm taking your cat," I told him, "and I'm moving to New York."

FIVE

THE STRANGER

A few months after moving to New York, I got the assign-ment that flew me to Paris. I was lying in my bedroom in Brooklyn at 11 am, giving sleep a second chance. I had a pillow over my face to block out the sunlight, and I must have looked so strange. Like someone trying to suffocate herself.

That's when Zac called. "What are you doing on Friday? Do you want to go to Paris?"

I sat up so fast it startled the cat. "Are you fucking with me?" I asked, because fucking with people was one of his specialties.

"I can find someone else if you don't want to go," he said. All casual.

"No, of course I can go. Yes. I'm going."

I thought moments like this only happened in the movies. One minute, you are languishing in Hangoverland. The next minute, the world's greatest assignment is sitting in your lap.

Well, "world's greatest assignment" might be a stretch. Zac was an editor for an in-flight magazine, so it's not like I was being cold-called by *Esquire*. The story I wrote would end up in the mesh netting of an airline seat, nestled alongside *SkyMall* and laminated instructions on how to turn your chair into a flotation device.

And the story itself was kind of silly. I was to interview the host of a popular reality dating show, shooting its eighth season in Paris. It was odd that the magazine wanted to fly me across the Atlantic to meet a guy whose claim to fame was the phrase "This is your final rose." But when someone offers to whisk you away to Europe on their dime, here is what you don't do: Ask questions. I was a freelance writer trying to make a living in New York City, for God's sake. I would have written a story for Downy Fabric Softener's internal newsletter.

"I'm going to Paris," I told the guys at the bodega where I bought cat food and smokes.

"Ooooh," they said, which was exactly the right response.

After only three months in the city, I was dangerously low on funds. But the magazine had authorized $1,000 spending money—a thousand dollars for two days!—which made me feel like I was standing in one of those game-show booths where $20 bills swirl like a tornado around you.

I was nervous about the plane ride. I'm a clutcher of armrests, a spinner of catastrophes. I have terrible control issues when it comes to letting someone pilot me across a vast and churning ocean. A point arrives in every flight when I fight the urge to bolt into the aisle and scream, "We're in the clouds, people! This can't last!" But I popped my sleeping pill and drank two vials of wine. Drinking on a plane is a line-item veto in the "never drink alone" rule book. Everyone drinks alone on a plane. We drink alone, together.

MY FIRST DAY in Paris went off without a hitch. I was staying at a hotel in the 14th arrondissement, in a residential area on the Left Bank not far from Luxembourg Gardens. It was a nice place: a bright foyer with high ceilings and marbled columns strung up with Christmas lights. The arrangements had been made by the magazine. All I had to do was show up.

"Your key, mademoiselle," said the man at the reception desk, handing me a plastic card.

I played tourist for the afternoon. Took the Metro to the Eiffel Tower, got my hands gooey with a chocolate crêpe, and walked across the park, feeling like a girl trailing ribbons in her wake. I found a cozy café tucked away on a quiet street and ordered a glass of bordeaux. It was cheaper than coffee. Two euros. Another one of the line-item vetoes in the "never drink alone" rule book is that you're allowed to drink alone while traveling. Who else could possibly join you? I loved drinking alone in distant bars, staying on speaking terms with my own solitude.

The wine was good. Sustaining. I sometimes wonder if I'd grown up in a culture lacking the padlocks of Puritan restrictions, then maybe I wouldn't have fetishized it so much. America, land of shot specials and beer bongs. No sense of moderation.

I read once that a famous magazine editor had a glass of champagne with every lunch. One glass. And I thought it was the classiest thing ever. I wanted that. The crystal flute, with its feminine curves and ding-ding-ding. The bubbles reaching up to kiss my nose as my lips approached the glass.

And so I sipped my one glass of red wine. Just one. And I let it roll along the sandpaper of my tongue. And the wine was better this way. Tiny sips. And it floated through my bloodstream like a warm front. And it would not be an overstatement to say this felt like the very point of existence. To savor each moment.

Then I ordered another glass.

I MET THE reality show host and his wife that night in a crowded square on the Right Bank. They had a toddler and an adorable baby, and they struggled to maneuver the stroller over the cobbled streets, even as we remarked how charming it was. The magazine profile was supposed to show how awesome it was to bring your kids to Paris, but I suspected the host and his wife would give an arm for a Babies "R" Us and a minivan.

The host was small and good-looking in a generic way. I expected to dislike him. In fact, I wanted to dislike him, because he was in charge of the world's dumbest social experiment. But he and his wife were quite lovely. Years later, when the tabloids reported their split, I actually thought: *But they seemed so happy.* As if I knew anything.

We took a seat at an Italian restaurant, ordered a bottle of red wine, and began the interview. My questions were not what you would call probing.

"Why did you decide to film this season in Paris?"

He cleared his throat. He smiled.

They had chosen Paris because it is the world's most romantic city. Anyone could fall in love in Paris. Everyone did! As the host spoke, I watched the season's sizzle reel unfold in my mind: candlelit dinners along the Champs-Élysée, helicopters flying above the Arc de Triomphe set to the swelling sounds of a power ballad, the corny accordion music leading us to commercial break.

I loved to rant about that show back when it debuted in 2002.

Those brainless women with their dripping bikini bodies and their Stepford smiles, scheming to marry a man they'd only just met. What kind of self-loathing idiot would watch this tripe?

The answer, it turned out, was me. Because a few years later, I flipped it on one evening and realized such vapid entertainment was a great way to unplug my mind. Anna started watching it, too, and we called each other afterward to complain. Untangling the mysteries of desire can be a terrific past time. *Why did he choose her? What was she thinking?* We might have talked more about those dopey bachelors than Anna's actual boyfriend, who became her husband that year.

After the interview, the TV host invited me back to their apartment. They had a bottle of wine they'd been meaning to open, and he and I drained it as his wife put the kids to bed. How many nights had I spent like this, sinking into some conversation with a man who was not my husband while his wife washed the dinner dishes, tended to the kids, and shushed us when our voices got too loud?

His wife plopped herself down beside us and yawned.

"Is there another bottle?" he asked, and she stared at him with red-rimmed eyes. She nodded slowly.

"I should go," I said, and she agreed with me a bit too quickly.

I hopped in a cab at 10 pm, and I was in that happy place where you feel impenetrable to harm. I loved talking to cabdrivers when I was like this; those impromptu conversations were one of my favorite parts of living in New York. I would hop in their Yellow Cab and perch myself up by the clear plastic divider, and I would scrutinize their names, their faces, trying to divine the landscapes that had shaped them.

"You're from Senegal," I would say, and the guy would laugh. No way. Not Senegal. Totally wrong.

"You're from the Ukraine," I would say, and the guy would gasp with recognition. How did I know that? Why was I so good at this?

My Paris cabbie didn't know much English. But he let me smoke in his cab, so I loved him. I was watching the cherry of my cigarette leave tracers across my line of vision. We zipped past tall white buildings that looked like wedding cakes in the peripheral blur. When he slammed on the brakes, I went hurtling onto the floorboard, my shin slamming against a piece of hard plastic.

He whipped around. "You OK?"

Later, I would find a throbbing bruise on my shin. But in the cab, I couldn't feel much at all. "I'm fine," I told him, hoisting myself back up and crossing my legs in the seat. "I'm great."

THE NEXT DAY I woke up early, full of possibility. I made a short appearance at the reality host's photo shoot near the Sacré-Cœur. His family posed on the butte Montmartre trying to look like they weren't freezing.

"I was paying for that last bottle this morning," he told me.

"Oh, I know," I said. I didn't feel that bad, but I liked the camaraderie of the hangover.

"Did you do anything else last night?"

"Nah," I said, omitting the two glasses of wine I had at the hotel bar.

I left them on the frigid hill, feeling nearly guilty for how easy this assignment had been. I had an entire day to myself in Paris. Should I go to the Louvre? Walk along the Seine? Instead I went back to my hotel, curled up in the fluffy white bed that felt so safe, and took a nap.

⁓

IT WAS DARK when I woke up. This was my last night in Paris, and I had dinner plans with a friend and a hefty per diem burning a hole in my pocket. I made myself extra-glamorous that night. I straight-ironed my hair and wore the black corset top that erased 15 of my extra 30 pounds.

My friend Meredith lived in an apartment a few blocks from my hotel. I met her when she worked at the *New York Times*, but she had since moved to Paris to work for the *International Herald Tribune*.

"I'm having a cognac," Meredith said as we stood in her kitchen. Cognac was an after-dinner drink, she conceded, but it was one of those days when 9 pm needed to arrive sooner. "Would you like one?"

I'd never had cognac before. But I was trying to be more refined. I'd started ordering high-end vodkas in Manhattan clubs where labels mattered. I'd been drinking Patrón tequila, and I liked to inform anyone who would listen how tequila was intended to be enjoyed slowly, not knocked back in one gulp.

"I'd love one, thanks." Her apartment was very *Architectural Digest*. The first floor had a glass ceiling, and if you looked through it, you could see the second-story skylight, and beyond that the stars. I wondered how many reality hosts I'd have to interview each month to afford a place like this.

I sat on the midcentury modern couch, rocking the snifter back and forth. I took a sip, and flames ripped down my throat. *Goddamn.* Why hadn't I been drinking this all my life? The buzz was warm and total. *Cognnnnnnaaac.* I liked the voluptuous sound. Two syllables, so much music. Meredith asked if I wanted another glass, and I hesitated for the briefest second. It was my last night in Paris. I had to say yes.

We ate dinner in Montparnasse at a restaurant that had once been Fitzgerald's favorite. Meredith worried it was a bit touristy, but I was excited to roll around in Lost Generation history. Art deco fixtures, high ceilings, white tablecloths. Meredith ordered a bottle of wine in fluent French, and I pretty much fell in love with her.

Did I blurt this out at the table? "I'm a little bit in love with you." I might have. I made such pronouncements all the time when I was lit, because most women walked around with their self-esteem around their ankles, and I felt a duty to help them lift it up. *You are really pretty. Did I ever tell you about the time you ordered the wine in perfect French?* Alcohol turned all my jealousy into buttercream.

We ordered oysters. We ordered escargot. Everything Meredith suggested, I responded with a hell yeah. The booze made me hyper. My foot was jostling, a motor without an off switch. And I drank to calm myself, as much as I drank to keep myself revved.

"This food is amazing," I told her, though even Spaghetti-Os tasted good when I was drunk.

The waiter came to offer dessert, and Meredith and I gave each other a conspiratorial look. *Two more cognacs, please.*

It was well past 11 when the check arrived, and we had burned through half a pack of cigarettes. I threw my credit card on the table without even looking at the total.

"I can't let you pay for all this," Meredith said, and I winked at her. "Don't worry. I'm not."

We tumbled into a cab. And here is where the night starts to stutter and skip. I see Meredith in the cab, the bundle of her scarf around her face. It's cold, and we are huddled together now, too drunk to care about our thighs pressed against each other. Good friends now. Old friends now. I see the red blur of the meter, a fuzzy dot in the corner. The baffling matter of euros. *What the fuck are all these coins?*

I'm pretty sure Meredith says, "I'm going to walk home from your hotel. I need the fresh air." We must have hugged good-bye. *I had such a good time. Let's do this again.* But that's not how it happens in my memory. In my memory, we're standing there, talking, and then—she's gone. Spliced from the scene. November leaves scuttling down the empty sidewalk near midnight in Paris. And I turn toward the rotating glass door, and I walk inside.

That tall guy behind the concierge desk. I've seen him before.

"How was your evening, mademoiselle?" His voice is almost comically low. A basso profundo, my mother would say.

"Excellent," I say. No slur in my voice. Nailed it. Slick floors like this can be dastardly in heels, and I've suffered a few spills in my time. Walking along, perfectly upright, and then *boom*. Face against the floor. I wave to the concierge, a good-night parting. Nice people here. Look at that: I made it all the way through the lobby without a slip.

And then the curtain descends. You know what happens next. Actually, neither of us does.

⁓

I USED TO have nightmares I was thrust onstage in the middle of a play, with no clue what I was supposed to say. In another version of the dream, I memorized lines for the wrong play, and nothing I said synced up with the characters onstage. I would wake up in my bed, collarbone slick, sheets in a noose around my legs. Later I discovered these were textbook anxiety dreams, which made me feel comforted, but lame. Even my subconscious was a cliché.

I used to tell myself, when I woke from those dreams, spooked and fog-brained: This could never happen. People never get to opening night without knowing the name of the play. This is just a catastrophe scenario, fired off by neurons. It isn't real. And yet, when the curtains opened up in my mind that night in Paris, and I was in bed with a guy I didn't even remember meeting, this is what I said:

> **ME**: I should go.
> **HIM**: You just said you wanted to stay.

It's strange to me how calm I remained. I was still wrapped in the soothing vapors of the cognac, no clue where I was but not particularly concerned. *I'll figure this out.*

I was pretty sure this was my hotel. I recognized the swirly brown carpet, the brushed-steel light fixtures. The bed had the same fluffy white sheets. But the oddest ideas drifted through my head. I thought maybe this guy was my boyfriend. I thought maybe he was the man I came to Paris to interview. It was like coming out of a very deep sleep and dragging the upside-down logic of dreams into real life. As though I woke up kissing a pillow, but the pillow happened to be slightly balding with kind eyes.

The panic started when I noticed the time. It was almost 2 am.

"Shit, my flight leaves in a few hours," I said.

Actually, the flight wasn't until 11 am, but I understood there was not nearly enough time between then and now. The awfulness of my circumstances began to dawn on me.

I dug my tights out of a ball at the foot of the bed and slapped my bra on so fast the eyeteeth were crooked. I hopped and stumbled as I zipped up my boots. I was knocking over things, shit clattering behind me. Sensation was returning to me in stages. Strange body parts felt sore. Later, it would sting when I peed.

"This was fun," I said.

He was lying in bed, one arm stretched out as though I were still in the cradle of his arms. His hand lifted in the casual, shrugging gesture of a person who hasn't been given a choice.

"Good-bye, I guess," he said.

I closed the door, and the click of the lock's tongue in the groove brought me such relief. The sound of a narrow escape.

I was on my way to the elevator when I realized: I did not have my purse.

WHEN I SAY I did not have my purse, I didn't give a shit about my actual purse, a black vinyl bag with stitching that had already started to unravel. But I did not have my wallet. I did not have my passport. I did not have my money, my driver's license, my room card, the keys to my loft back in Brooklyn.

I did not have my way back home.

I turned around and stared at the line of doorways behind me. *Shit. They all look the same. Which one?* It was powerfully unfair. Forgetting something that *just fucking happened.*

It made no sense. A woman can spend half her life haunted by a sixth grader's taunt that took place in 1985. But she can have absolutely no idea what happened 20 seconds ago.

Stop. Stay calm. Think. I retraced my steps. Had I passed five rooms on my way to the elevator? Or four? I searched for pointy heel indentions in the red carpet, which was covered with whorls like the forked tongue of a snake. I found nothing, but

I kept searching for any trail of string. *Did I pass that Emergency sign? What about this room service tray sitting by the door?*

Deductive reasoning suggested I had come from the corner room, because his window was larger than mine and the room more of an L shape, so I walked back down the hall. I took a deep breath and knocked on the door. Mine was the tentative knock of the thoroughly unconvinced. The "pardon me" knock. The "I know you're busy" knock.

Nothing happened. No one came.

I looked at the door beside it. On second thought, maybe it was this one. Perhaps the room wasn't L-shaped, so much as the furniture was rearranged. Another knock, louder this time.

Nothing, no one.

I wondered if he was in the shower. Maybe he had already passed out, snoring in the same position I left him. People who've been drinking can be so hard to rouse.

I went back to the original door. I took a deep breath, and I pounded on it. I pounded with both fists, and I tried very hard not to think about what might happen if I had the wrong door. A guy staring through the fish-eye while his wife asks, "Who is it, honey?"

Nothing happened. No one came.

I looked down the hallway, at the doors lined up before me. Was it me, or did they stretch into infinity? I clutched my hair, then doubled over in a silent scream.

I slumped down the wall and sat in the patch of space between two doors. I closed my eyes and stayed still for a very long time. I wanted so many things in that moment. I wanted to call Anna. I wanted to call my boyfriend, but he wasn't my boyfriend anymore. I wanted Bubba, and the calming way he curled up on my chest, paws barely touching my neck, so I could feel the tiny patter of his heart and the boom in my own rib cage. Almost like our hearts were having a conversation with each other.

I don't know how long I sat in that hallway. Ten minutes, ten years.

When I finally stood up, I had a plan.

IN COLLEGE, WE joked about the "walk of shame." It was the term for the bleary-eyed stagger of Sunday morning—when you had to pass coeds who raised their eyebrows at your tangled hair and your one broken heel. The great thing about a term like "walk of shame" is that its cleverness leaches the embarrassment from the act. To endure a walk of shame was not shameful anymore, because you were participating in a rite of passage, familiar to any well-lived life. Like so much of our vernacular— wasted, smashed, obliterated, fucked up—I never thought much about it.

But heading down to the concierge desk in the middle of the night was a true walk of shame. I swiped a knuckle under each lid as I rode down in the elevator. I straightened my wool skirt. I tried to look like a woman who had not just emerged from a hole in the ground.

"Bonjour," I said to the concierge. My voice was chased by those hollow echoes that come in the wee hours of the night.

"Good evening," he said. "What can I do for you?"

Above the desk, a series of clocks kept time around the world. It was only 8:30 pm back in New York, which sounded so safe and far away.

"I left my purse in someone's room," I said.

"Not a problem," he said, and began tapping on the computer. "What room was it?"

I shook my head. I traced a figure eight on the counter with my index finger. "I don't know."

"Not a problem," he said. More tapping. "What was the guest's name?"

A tear slipped down my cheek, and I watched it splat. "I don't know."

He nodded, his mouth an expressionless line. But I could see the pity in his eyes. He felt sorry for me. And somehow this pebble of sympathy was enough to shatter my fragile reserve. I crumpled into tears.

"Don't cry," he said. He took my hand. His fingers were dry and cold and they swallowed mine. "It's going to be OK," he said.

And I believed him, because I needed to.

People talk about the horrible things strangers do to you when you are drunk, but my experience has mostly been the opposite. I have been the recipient of so much unsolicited kindness. The bartender who helps me track down the shoes I threw under a table. The woman who slips the glass of water under the bathroom stall where my head hangs over a toilet rim with a fishing line of drool stretching from my lips to the water. *Honey, I've been there.*

And then there were my friends, my actual friends, who would walk me up the stairs to my bedroom. Who poured me into taxis and texted with me until I was home. They did it for me, and I would do it for them. The golden rule of a lush's life. Be kind to drunk people, for every one of them is fighting an enormous battle.

"Is it possible this gentleman is the one you were talking to at the bar tonight?" the concierge asked.

And there it was, finally. My first clue.

OF COURSE. OF course I'd gone to the hotel bar. It was located directly off the lobby. *Pass the concierge and veer to the right.* It's where I'd gone after my interview on the first night, when I got back to my hotel and wasn't ready to concede the good times just yet.

Did the guy pick me up? Did I pick him up? Was "picking" even the right verb? The bar was small, a few leather booths and a smattering of wooden tables. Striking up a conversation in a place like this would be exceedingly easy. There's an hour when finding someone in a bar to sleep with doesn't require a clever line so much as a detectable pulse.

> HIM: Come here often?
> ME: You bet.
> HIM: Wanna fuck?
> ME: You bet.
> HIM: Should I tell you my name first?
> ME: That's OK. I won't remember it.

I was embarrassed by my aggressive sexuality when I drank. It didn't feel like me. And after a blackout, I would torture myself thinking of the awful things I might have said or done. My mind became an endless loop of what scared me the most.

At the concierge desk, I didn't have time to indulge in such fantasy. I pretended to remember the guy. Anything to bluff my way out of this mess.

"Yes," I told him, clapping my hands together. "That is definitely the guy. So you saw me with him tonight?"

He smiled. "Of course."

Hallelujah. I had a witness.

He handed me a new key to my room. He told me he would figure out the guy's name but that he might need an hour or two. "I don't want you to worry anymore," he said. "Go rest."

"Hey, what's your name?" I asked.

"Johnson," he said.

"I'm Sarah," I told him, and I took his hand with both of mine. A double-decker handshake. "Johnson, you're the hero of my story tonight."

"Not a problem," he said, and flashed a smile.

As I headed toward the elevator, I felt like a new woman. I had a chance to restore order, to correct the insanity of the night. Johnson would find the guy's name. I would meet the guy downstairs, suffer the indignity of small talk, then take my stuff and bolt. No, better yet, Johnson would knock on the guy's door and retrieve the purse himself. I didn't care how it happened, just that it happened. It was all going to be OK.

I walked back into my room. And there, to the left of the entrance, on an otherwise unremarkable shelf, was a sack of vinyl, openmouthed and drooping. Holy shit: my purse.

⁓

A WOMAN TOLD me a story once about folding her clothes in a blackout. She woke up, and her room was clean. How bizarre is that? But I understood how, even in a state of oblivion, you fight to keep order.

I had lost so many things that fall in New York. Sunglasses. Hats, scarves, gloves. I could have outfitted an orphanage with the items I left behind in taxicabs. But what amazed me was how many things I did not lose, even when my eyes had receded back into my skull. I never lost my cell phone. I never lost my keys. I once woke up with the refrigerator door flapping open but my good pearl earrings placed neatly beside the sink, their tricky backs slipped back onto their stems.

Part of this was simple survival. You could not be a woman alone in the world without some part of you remaining vigilant. I was a woman who tripped over sidewalks and walked into walls, but I was also a woman who, at the end of the evening, held on to her valuables like they were a dinosaur egg.

How did my purse get in my room? This new evidence was forcing me to reevaluate the story I'd already settled on. I suppose I might have dropped the purse off on my way to the guy's hotel room. But a side trip like that was a serious break in the action that didn't track with a drunk's impulsive style. The more likely scenario is that I went upstairs first, decided my room was entirely too quiet, and then headed back to the bar for company, leaving my purse behind. A woman locking up her diamond ring before she leaps into the sea.

I called the front desk. "You're never going to believe this," I told Johnson. "My purse is in my room."

"I told you this would work out," he said.

"And you were right."

I changed into my pajamas and curled into a fetal position under the covers. An empty bed had never been so divine. Maybe I should have been relieved, but I had the haunted shivers of a woman who felt the bullet whiz past her face. Now that my crisis was resolved, I could start beating myself up for the ways I had failed. All that I could have lost.

This was a familiar crouch—staring at the ceiling at 3 am, lashing myself. Such a wretched place to be. Alone in the dark, with your own misery.

The phone rang.

"I found a leather jacket in the bar," Johnson said. "Do you think it's yours?"

And here comes the part of the story I wish I didn't remember.

⁓

JOHNSON STANDS IN my doorway. He's so tall. He must be six two. My leather jacket is draped over his arm like a fresh towel. I stand there with my hand on the door and wonder how much to tip him.

"Can I come in?" he asks, and there is not an ounce of me that wants him inside my room, but he was so helpful to me earlier, and I can't scheme quickly enough to rebuff him.

I step back from the door and give him entry. I'm still thinking about the tip. Would five euros be enough? Would a hundred?

He closes the door and walks to my bed. It's not far from the entryway, but each step breaches a great chasm. "You broke my heart when you cried earlier tonight," he says, sitting down on the mattress. He's only a few feet from me, and I remain with my back pressed against the wall.

"I know, I'm sorry about that," I say, and I think: *Who is manning the desk right now? Are we going to get in trouble?*

He leans forward on the bed, resting his elbows on his knees. "I was thinking, a beautiful woman like you should not be crying," he says, and puts out his hand for me to take. I'm not sure what to do, but I walk over to him, as if on autopilot, and let my hand hang limply against his fingertips. "You are very beautiful," he says.

I blink and breathe deeply through my nostrils. Fucking Christ. It is a compliment that makes me want to wither away. I have spent years chasing after compliments, with the ridiculous hope that every man in the universe would find me beautiful.

And now a man arrives at 3:30 am to tell me I have succeeded in my pathetic, girlish hopes and dreams, and I want to crush him. I want to scream.

"Thanks," I say.

"I saw you Saturday night when you came in," he says. I stare at the floor, wondering how to get my hand back. I'm not sure what makes me angrier: that he will not leave, or that I will not ask him to. For the millionth time, I'm enraged by a man's inability to read my mind. *Look at how I'm standing here. Can't you see how revolting I find you?*

"I'm glad I could take care of you," he says, and he brings my hand to his lips.

"Johnson, I'm really tired," I say. "It's been a really long day." I want him to leave so badly my stomach aches.

I think: *If tell him to go, he'll probably stand up politely and walk out of the room without saying more than a few words.* So why don't I? Do I feel I owe him something? That I can't turn him away? That he'll be mad at me? *What do I feel?*

He pulls me toward him, and we kiss.

The kiss is neither bad nor good. I consider it a necessary penance. I can't explain it. How little I care. Zapping back to my life in the middle of sex with a stranger seems to have raised the bar on what I can and cannot allow. All I keep thinking is: *This doesn't matter.* All I keep thinking is: *It will be easier this way.*

He tugs me toward the bed, and my body moves before my brain tells it differently. I let him run his hands along me, and he strokes my hair. He kisses my nose, now wet with tears he does not ask about. He moves his large, rough hands over the steep slope of my fleshy sides, up along my breast, nudging down my top and gently sucking on my nipple.

And the confounding part is how good this feels. It shouldn't feel this way. My skin should be all bugs and slithering worms. But the truth is I like being held. I like not being alone any-more. None of this makes sense in my mind, because I don't want to be here, but I can't seem to leave. I don't understand it. What accumulation of grief and loneliness could bring me to this place, where I could surrender myself to the hands of a stranger? Who is this person in the hotel room? And I don't mean Johnson. I mean me.

We lie in the bed, and he strokes my face, my body. I can feel him hard against me, but he never asks for more.

At 4 am, I push Johnson out the door. I climb into my bed and cry. Huge howling sobs, and I feel a small amount of comfort knowing the story exists only in my memory bank and that I do not need to deposit it in anyone else's. This whole episode can stay a secret.

✦

REAL DRUNKS WAIT and watch for the moment they hit bottom. Your face is forever hurtling toward a brick wall, but you hope that you can smash against it and still walk away. That you will be scared but not destroyed. It's a gamble. How many chances do you want to take? How many near misses are enough?

As I lay in my hotel bed, covers pulled up to my neck, I felt the gratitude of a woman who knows, finally, she is done.

But I drank on the plane ride home. And I drank for five more years.

SIX

THE LIFE YOU'VE ALWAYS WANTED

My apartment in New York was on the southern edge of Williamsburg, back when rents were almost reasonable. I had a view of the bridge into Manhattan, strung up with lights like a Christmas tree. I had painted my living room in red candy cane stripes. When Stephanie came over to visit shortly after I moved in, she said, "You're never leaving this place." And I was so proud to have impressed her for a change.

Paris had been devastating, but also a onetime deal. A private disaster is easy to rewrite for public consumption. "How was Paris?" / "Amazing!" And people nodded, because how else would Paris be? Besides, I had better views in front of me. Here I was. I was here. *A writer in New York*: the phrase that compensated for nearly anything.

Dreamers plan their lives long before they live them, and by the fall of 2005, mine was finally catching up to the script. The details were a little off. I wasn't 23 when I moved to the big city;

I was 31. I wasn't exactly writing *Catcher in the Rye*. I was writing hack profiles and advance blurbs for *Lego Star Wars: The Video Game*. And I wasn't nestled in the tree-lined Valhalla of literary Brooklyn. I was scraping by in a borough where razor wire was giving way to ironic T-shirts.

But I loved my big, rambling apartment. The owner of the building was a small Dominican woman in her late 50s, with a tight bun and a stern demeanor. She spoke little English, and I refused to speak Spanish with her, because I didn't want to cede what little comfort zone I had, so we were reduced to curt nods in the hallway. Her entire family lived in the building. Her heavyset single daughter, who stopped by to discuss noise complaints. (I had a few.) Her sketchy son, who smoked on the front steps while talking on a cell phone. Her six-year-old twin granddaughters, with heads of kinky curls.

"Is your cat home?" one of them would ask from the hallway, lisping through her gap teeth. This question would crack me up. As though sometimes my cat were at work.

My first year was mostly good. Promising. And having finally settled the bullet points of my life, I was ready to finesse the details. Less furniture pulled from curbs. Better skin care products. A little personal improvement.

I had this great idea: I should learn to cook. My mother had tried to teach me a few times in my early 20s, but I blew her off. *Women don't need to know this stuff anymore*, I told her, like she was instructing me in stenography.

But 12 months in the city had made me question this tack. Too much of my paycheck was being handed over to deliverymen. I also hoped cooking might forge a healthier connection to food and drink, which I badly needed. How had I determined that *not* learning a skill was a position of power?

My cooking experiments began with promise. Me, in that empty kitchen, slicing and dicing like a mature, grown-up adult person. I would open a bottle of wine to enjoy while I did prep work. But wine made me chatty, so I would call friends back in Texas. And I'd get so engrossed in the conversation, I didn't want to cook anymore. I'd lose my appetite after the second glass, and I'd bundle the food and stuff it back into the refrigerator, trading asparagus spears for half a dozen Parliaments by the window.

When the bottle was drained, I'd slip out to the bodega and pick up two 24-ounce Heinekens. The equivalent of four beers, which I had titrated to be the perfect amount: just enough to get me to the edge without pushing me over. (The only recipe I knew.) Around midnight, when hunger came on like a clawing beast, I'd throw some pasta in a pot of boiling water, slather it with butter and salt, and devour it while I watched cable. Didn't Wolfgang Puck start this way?

My friend Stephanie actually married a chef from the Food Network. Bobby. They lived in an elegant Manhattan apartment—two stories, with a standing bar and a pool table upstairs. Visiting her was like stepping into the Life You've Always Wanted, but the thing about Stephanie was, she wanted to share it. She paid for our dinners, floated my cab fare, and made the world lighter with a million other tiny gestures that had nothing to do with money.

Stephanie was in a Broadway play in the spring, and I went to the opening-night party at Bobby's Midtown bistro, which was like taking straight shots of glamour. Naomi Watts was there. Supporting actors from *Sex and the City*. I stood in line for the bathroom behind Bernadette Peters (from *Annie!*), and I had a cigarette with the guy who starred in the second season of *The Wire*. I texted a friend, "I just bummed a smoke from Frank

Sobotka!" In our circle, this was like splitting an ice-cream sundae with Julia Roberts.

Kids who crave fame often imagine New York will be like this. One big room full of celebrities and cocktails. Stephanie's party wasn't too far from my own childhood fantasies. Except this time, I was in it.

I went back to Bobby's restaurant as often as I could after that. One night in the fall, I was having a drink there with a bunch of Stephanie's friends, including a saucy redhead I liked. Around 8 pm, our friends peeled off for dinner plans and more responsible lives, and the redhead turned to me.

"You want to go to another bar?" she asked.

And that was an easy question. "Sure."

We rambled on to a trendy spot in Hell's Kitchen and bonded over the miseries of the single life while slurping down $17 martinis. I remember what they cost, because I had to do quick math. *How many of these can I squeeze on my last working credit card and still afford the cab ride home?* The redhead had been out of work for a while, a fact she was very open about, and I couldn't figure out how she managed to stay in her Upper West Side apartment and afford $17 martinis. I wanted to ask her, but I never found a polite way to introduce the topic. So we sat there discussing our favorite sexual positions.

At midnight, we walked to the corner to catch a cab. My heels were in my hands, my bare feet slapping on the gummy sidewalk. By the time the taxi dropped me off at home, I had an insane hunger. I boiled water on the stove and threw in some pasta. I flopped down on the futon and turned on that VH1 show where talking-head comedians make fun of Milli Vanilli and Teddy Ruxpin.

The next part is confusing. A banging at the door. The land-lord's sketchy son with a fire extinguisher in his hands. Gray smoke churning over the stove. The earsplitting beeping of the alarm.

"Open the window," he said. Sweat was dripping off his face as he worked to secure the kitchen. I stood behind him, arms dangling at my sides.

"Your alarm's been going off for half an hour," he said, and he moved the pot of charred spaghetti stalks off the burner.

"I must have fallen asleep," I said, a much gentler phrase than "passed out." But I wondered if they knew. Surely they'd seen all the cans and bottles in my recycling bin.

Ten minutes later, the landlord stood in my kitchen. She was in a blue robe, with her arms crossed. "You try to burn down my apartment," she said.

"Oh no," I said, startled by the accusation and hoping it was a glitch in translation. "It was an accident. I'm so sorry."

I couldn't go back to sleep that night. At 5 am, before the sun rose, I decided to take a walk. I walked across the Williamsburg Bridge, and I walked through the trash-strewn streets of the Lower East Side, past the discount stores with their roll-down metal gates locked shut, and through the tidy sidewalk cafés of Chelsea, and into the din of Midtown. If my feet hurt, I didn't notice. I needed forward motion. I needed to keep in front of my shame. I was near the zoo at Central Park when the landlord's daughter called me.

"When your lease is up in April, we'd like you to move out," she said.

"OK, I'm sorry," I said.

She must have hated making that call. She must have hated

being the translator of Difficult Information. "Listen, you're a good person, but my mom is really upset. The building is old. Her granddaughters live there. The whole place could have gone up in flames."

"I understand," I said, though it felt like an overreaction to a genuine mistake. *I fell asleep*, I kept thinking. *How could spaghetti smoke burn down your building?* But underneath those defensive voices, the knowledge I was wrong. To cast the event as anyone's whoopsie was to exclude key evidence. Like the part where I drank three martinis, two beers—and passed out.

"I was thinking about buying your mother a plant," I said. "Or maybe flowers. Do you know what kind she likes?"

"I don't think that's a good idea," she said.

"Oh," I said, because I thought everyone liked flowers.

"I think the better idea is if you don't say anything, and you move out in April."

I walked all the way up to Washington Heights, up to 181st Street, where my friend Lisa lived. We'd met at the Austin paper, and she was one of the first people to convince me I could make a living in New York. I slept on her couch during my first month in the city, and I used to drift off, listening to her and her husband laugh in their bedroom, and I would think about how I would like that one day. Lisa and Craig were leading candidates for the greatest people I knew, and if you are ever as low as I was that morning, I hope you can walk far enough to get to Lisa's doorstep.

She and I pulled a couple chairs outside and sat quietly in the sunshine. I stared off at the George Washington Bridge, the blue sky behind it. My lips were trembling. "I think I'm going to have to quit drinking," I said, and she said, "I know. I'm sorry. I love you."

And I quit drinking. For four days.

I HAD THIS great idea: I should get a job. Freelancing came with freedom, but maybe what I required was a cage. I also needed a regular paycheck. I was $10K in the hole to credit card companies. And I had neglected to pay a hefty IRS bill. Twice.

I got a job as a writer and editor at an online magazine called *Salon*. The gig came with full benefits, perhaps the most important being hope. I looked at each new change—every geographic move, every shuffle of my schedule—as a reason to believe I might finally reform bad habits. Drinkers have an unlimited supply of 4 am epiphanies and "no, really, I've got it this time" speeches.

But no, really, *I had it this time*. One of my first *Salon* essays was about confronting my credit card debt, which had gotten so out of control I had to borrow money from my parents. That was a low moment, but it came with a boost of integrity. A free tax attorney helped me calculate the amount I owed to the IRS—$40,000— and put me on a payment plan. My commitment was seven years, which made me feel like the guy from *Shawshank Redemption*, tunneling out of prison with a spoon. But finally, I was coming clean.

The credit card debt story introduced a new problem, however. The day after the piece ran, an intern stopped by my desk. "What do you think about the comments on your piece?" she asked. "Pretty insane, huh?"

"Totally," I said, though I hadn't actually read them. That night, fortified by a bottle of wine, I waded into the comments. There were hundreds. Some people scolded me for my debt. Some mocked me for not having *enough* debt. But they mostly agreed this was a worthless article written by a loser.

My mother used to tell me I was my own worst critic. Clearly, she wasn't reading the comments.

I began losing my nerve. I started second-guessing everything—not just my writing, but my editing. The Internet was a traffic game, scary and unfamiliar to me, and I felt torn between the real journalist I wanted to be and the snake-oil salesman who had to turn a fluff piece into a viral sensation. I woke up writing headlines, rearranging words like Scrabble tiles for maximum effect.

I started drinking at home more. A way to save money. A reward for a challenging day. I switched up the bodegas each time, so none of the guys behind the counter would catch on.

When the first layoff hit *Salon* in the fall of 2008, I was spared. But I was frightened by the tremors under my feet. My boss told me the names of the people who were let go, and I cried like they'd been shot. *Those people are so nice*, I kept thinking. As if that had anything to do with it. As if a global financial disaster is going to select for kindness.

The more unstable the world became, the more earned my reckless drinking felt. After a night out with friends, I would stop by the bodega for a six-pack. Sunday nights became a terrible reckoning. I would lie under my duvet, and I would drink white wine, watching *Intervention*, coursing with the low-down misery that another Monday was on its way.

I should quit. I knew I needed to quit. After a doozy I would wake up and think "Never again," and by 3 pm I would think, "But maybe today."

~~~~~

I HAD THIS great idea: I should go into therapy. My parents agreed to shoulder most of the bill, and I felt guilty, because I knew the strain it would cause. But even worse would be not getting help at all.

My therapist was a maternal woman, with a nod I trusted.

Whenever I thought about lying to her, I tried to envision flushing a hundred-dollar bill down the toilet.

"What about rehab?" she asked.

Eesh. That was a little dramatic.

"I can't," I said. I couldn't leave my cat. I couldn't leave my colleagues. I couldn't afford it. If I was gonna do rehab, I wanted to be shipped off to one of those celebrity-studded resorts in Malibu, where you do Pilates and gorge on pineapple all day, not holed up a dingy facility with metal beds.

Still, I longed for some intervening incident to make me stop. Who doesn't want a deus ex machina? Some benevolent character to float down from the clouds and take the goddamn pinot noir out of your hands?

I had this great idea: I should try antidepressants. And another great idea: I should toss the antidepressants and join a gym. And another great idea: What about a juice cleanse? And another, and another.

My body was starting to break down. After an average bout of heavy drinking, I would wake up in the mornings feeling poisoned, needing to purge whatever was left in my stomach. I would kneel at the toilet, place two fingers down the back of my throat, and make myself vomit. Shower, go to work.

I had to quit. I would try for a few days, but I never got further than two weeks. I became paranoid I was going to lose my job. Whenever I sat down to write, the words wouldn't come. The pressure and the doubt and the stress could no longer be sipped away. I was completely blocked.

"I'm going to get fired," I told my boss one afternoon, freaking out over a late deadline.

"Look at me," she said. "You are not going to lose your job." And she was right.

But she lost hers. The second layoff came a few weeks later, in August of 2009, and when the list of the damned was read, my boss's name was on it, along with half the New York office. I couldn't believe it. All those months I was convinced I'd be axed, and I was one of the only survivors.

Why did they keep me? I'll never know. Maybe I was cheap. Maybe I was agreeable. Maybe my name never got pulled from the hat. I suspected my boss never let them see how much I was floundering. She protected me, and she got the pink slip. I was left with my job, my fear, and my guilt.

After work, I went straight to the bar. I had built up a week of sobriety at that point. But no way I was staying sober for this bullshit.

STEPHANIE WAS THE one who finally confronted me. She took me to dinner at a nice little Italian restaurant in Park Slope. She adjusted the napkin in her lap with pretty hands that displayed a gargantuan diamond.

"I need to talk to you," she said. The bugle call for a horrible conversation. She needed to talk to me because, at a gathering at her place, I burst into tears talking about the layoffs while we all smoked on the balcony. "You kind of freaked people out," she said, which stung, because I thought everyone had bonded that night.

She needed to talk to me because, at a recent dinner, I told the story of a hideous romantic breakup with such heart-wrenching detail that one of Stephanie's friends held my hand on the way back in the cab. That's how moved she'd been. Meanwhile, Stephanie diverted her sigh into her hair. She'd heard the story three times before.

For the past few months, I had been hearing about girls' dinners and group trips taken without me, and I thought, well, they probably knew I couldn't afford it. I tried not to get my feelings hurt. No biggie, it was cool.

But sitting across from Stephanie, I began to realize it was *not* cool. Something was badly wrong between us. And it wasn't some minor incident on the balcony, or a cab, but the long string of incidents that came before it. Discord is often an accumulation. A confrontation is like a cold bucket of water splashed on you at once, but what you might not realize is how long the bucket of water was building. Five drops, a hundred drops, each of them adding to the next, until one day—the bucket tips.

"I don't know what you want," she said. The words scraped her throat, which spooked me, because she was not a person whose composure faltered. "What do you want?"

And I thought: I want fancy trips and a house in the Hamptons and long delicate hands that show off a gargantuan diamond.

I thought: I want to not be having this conversation.

I thought: I want to not be abandoned by the people I love.

I thought: I want a fucking drink.

"I don't know," I said. She took my hand, and she did not let go for a long time. I wish I could say this was the end of my drinking. Instead, Stephanie and I didn't see each other for about a year.

What I told her at dinner was true, though. I did not know what I wanted. Or rather, I knew exactly what I wanted, which was to never have to face a day without alcohol and to never have to face the consequences of keeping it in my life. I wanted the impossible. This is the place of pinch and bargaining that greets you as you approach the end. You can't live with booze, and you can't live without it.

ONE MORE LAST great idea: I should move to Manhattan. Brooklyn was for kids, but the city was for adults. I moved in the middle of an ice storm, on December 31, 2009, just in time for a fresh start.

My studio was 250 square feet. I misjudged its size, having first seen the place without furniture. Living in a space that small was like stacking my belongings on the middle seat of an airplane. There was nowhere to sit but my bed, so I stayed under the covers and drank with the lights out and the door chained, like a blackout curtain drawn over my entire life. I stayed home most nights, because it kept me out of trouble. Sometimes I watched soft-core porn for no other reason than I was given free Showtime. I was down to mostly beer now. Beer was good to me. I have always relied on the kindness of Stella Artois.

Anna came to New York to visit me. She slept beside me on the bed in that teensy studio and never complained. She was five months' pregnant, with no luggage other than a small back-pack, and she glowed. I felt like a bloated wreck next to her. She had great ideas, too: Maybe I could eat healthier. Maybe more activity outdoors. She found a yoga studio in my neighborhood and brought back a schedule. I promised I'd try. But I was too far gone. There is a certain brokenness that cannot be fixed by all the downward dogs and raw juice in the world.

My therapist said to me, "I'm not sure it makes sense to keep doing these sessions if you're not going to stop drinking." I must have looked stricken, because she refined it. "I'm worried the work of therapy isn't going to help if you don't quit. Do you understand why I'm saying that?"

Yes, I understood: *Fuck off. Go away. Done with you.*

I did not want to give up therapy, any more than I wanted to give up my friends or the memories of my evenings, but the need to hold on to booze was primal. Drinking had saved me. When I was a child trapped in loneliness, it gave me escape. When I was a teenager crippled by self-consciousness, it gave me power. When I was a young woman unsure of her worth, it gave me courage. When I was lost, it gave me the path: that way, toward the next drink and everywhere it leads you. When I triumphed, it celebrated with me. When I cried, it comforted me. And even in the end, when I was tortured by all that it had done to me, it gave me oblivion.

Quitting is often an accumulation. Not caused by a single act but a thousand. Drops fill the bucket, until one day the bucket tips.

On the evening of June 12, 2010, I went to a friend's wedding reception in a Tribeca loft. It was lovely. I had red wine, and then I switched to white. I was sitting at a big round table near the window with a guy in a white dinner jacket and clunky black glasses. The last thing I remember seeing is his face, his mouth open in mid-laugh. And behind him, night.

I woke up in my bed the next morning. I didn't know how the reception ended or how I got home. Bubba was beside me, purring. Nothing alarming, nothing amiss. Just another chunk of my life, scooped out as if by a melon baller.

People who refuse to quit drinking often point to the status markers they still have. They make lists of things they have not screwed up yet: I still had my apartment. I still had my job. I had not lost my boyfriend, or my children (because I didn't have any to lose).

I took a bath that night, and I lay in the water for a long time, and I dripped rivers down my thighs and my pale white belly,

and it occurred to me for the first time that perhaps no real consequences would ever come to me. I would not end up in a hospital. I would not wind up in jail. Perhaps no one and nothing
would ever stop me. Instead, I would carry on like this, a hope-
less little lush in a space getting smaller each year. I had held on
to many things. But not myself.

I don't know how to describe the blueness that overtook me.
It was not a wish for suicide. It was an airless sensation that I
was already dead. The lifeblood had drained out of me.

I rose out of the bathtub, and I called my mother. A mother
was a good call to make before abandoning hope. And I said to
her the words I had said a thousand times—to friends, and to
myself, and to the silent night sky.

"I think I'm going to have to quit drinking," I told her.

And this time, I did.

BEGINNING

The closet in my Manhattan studio was just big enough to climb inside. I had to rearrange boxes and bags of old clothes, but if I cleared the ground like brush and squished my sleeping bag underneath me like a giant pillow, I could curl up in a ball compact enough to shut the closet door.

I don't know why it took me so long to figure this out. All those years I spent on the bed as the sun stabbed me through the blinds. Seeking cover under blankets and pillows, wearing silky blue eye masks like I was some '60s movie heroine. All those mornings I felt so exposed, but five feet away was a closet offering a feeling of total safety. My very own panic room.

I needed protection, because I had such turtle skin in those days. I knew quitting drinking would mean giving up the euphoria of the cork eased out of the bottle at 6 pm. What I did not expect is that I would feel so raw and threatened by the world. The clang and shove of strangers on the streets outside. The liquor stores lurking on every corner.

But you'd be surprised how manageable life feels when it has been reduced to a two-by-five-foot box. Notice how the body folds in on itself. Listen to the smooth stream of breath. Focus on the *ba-thunk* of the heart. That involuntary metronome. That low, stubborn drumbeat. Isn't it weird how it keeps going, even when you tell it to stop?

Sobriety wasn't supposed to be like this. I thought when I finally quit drinking for good, the universe would open its treasure chest for me. That only seemed fair, right? I would sacrifice the greatest, most important relationship of my existence— here I am, universe, sinking a knife into my true love's chest for you—and I would be rewarded with mountains of shimmering, clinking gold to grab by the fistful. I would be kicking down doors again. In badass superhero mode.

Instead, I woke up at 5 am each day, chest hammering with anxiety, and crawled into the closet for a few hours to shut out unpleasant voices. *When will I screw this up again? What failures lurk beyond these four walls?* I trudged through the day with shoulders slumped, every color flipped to gray scale. I spent evenings on my bed, arm draped over my face. Hangover posture. I didn't like the lights on. I didn't even like TV. It was almost as if, in absence of drinking blackouts, I was forced to create my own.

I had a few sources of comfort. I liked my cat. I liked food. I scarfed down ice cream, which was weird, because when I was drinking, I hated sweets. "I'll drink my dessert," I used to say, because sugar messed with my high. But now I devoured a pint of Häagen-Dazs in one sitting, and I didn't feel an ounce of guilt, because people quitting the thing they love get to eat whatever the fuck they want.

I built a bridge to midnight with peanut butter and chocolate. Four-cheese macaroni and tins of lasagna. Chicken tikka masala with extra naan, delivered in bags containing two forks. And if I made it to midnight, I won. Another day on the books: five, seven, eleven days down. Then I'd wake up at 5 am and start this bullshit all over again.

Back in my 20s—in that wandering place of travel and existential searching that unfolded between newspaper jobs—I briefly worked at a foster home for children with catastrophic illnesses. One of the babies did not have a brain, a fate I didn't even know was possible. He had a brain stem but not a brain, which allowed his body to develop even as his consciousness never did. And I would think about that baby when I climbed in the closet, because when you took off his clothes to change his diaper or bathe him he screamed and screamed, his tiny pink tongue darting about. Such simple, everyday transitions, but not to him. When you moved him, he lost all sense of where he was in the world. "It's like you've plunged him into an abyss," the nurse told me once as she wrapped him like a burrito. "That's why you swaddle him tight. It grounds him." She picked him back up again, and he was quiet and docile. The demons had scattered. And that's what the closet felt like to me. Without it, I was flailing in the void.

Not taking a drink was easy. Just a matter of muscle movement, the simple refusal to put alcohol to my lips. The impossible part was everything else. How could I talk to people? Who would I be? What would intimacy look like, if it weren't coaxed out by the glug-glug of a bottle of wine or a pint of beer? Would I have to join AA? Become one of those frightening 12-step people? How the fuck could I write? My livelihood, my identity, my purpose, my light—all extinguished with the tightening of a screw cap.

And yet. Life with booze had pushed me into that tight corner of dread and fear. So I curled up inside the closet, because it felt like being held. I liked the way the door smooshed up against my nose. I liked how the voices in my mind stopped chattering the moment the doorknob clicked. It was tempting to stay in there forever. To run out the clock while I lay there thinking about how unfair, and how terrible, and why me. But I knew one day, I would have to open the door. I would have to answer the only question that really matters to the woman who has found herself in the ditch of her own life.

How do I get out of here?

PART TWO

SEVEN

ISN'T THERE ANOTHER WAY?

I've never liked the part of the book where the main character gets sober. No more cheap sex with strangers, no more clattering around bent alleyways with a cigarette scattering ashes into her cleavage. *A sober life.* Even the words sound deflated. Like all the helium leaked out of your pretty red balloon.

In the first few weeks, though, I didn't actually know I had gotten sober. Have you ever broken up with a guy, like, 15 times? And each time you slam the door and throw his shit on the lawn and tell yourself, with the low voice of the newly converted: *No more.* But a few days pass, and you remember how his fingertips traced the skin on your neck and how your legs twined around him. And "forever" is a long time, isn't it? So you hope he never calls, but you also wait for him to darken your doorway at an hour when you can't refuse him, and it's hard to know which you would prefer. Maybe you need to break up *16* times. Or maybe— just *maybe*—this is the end.

That was my mind-set at 14 days. I kept a mental list of the order my friends would forgive me if I started drinking again. I called my mother when I got home from work every night. A way to tie myself to the mast from six to midnight.

"How are you doing?" she asked in a voice I deemed too chipper.

"Fine," I told her in a voice suggesting I was not. Our conversations were not awesome. I could feel her sweeping floodlights over the ground, searching for the right thing to say.

"Are you writing?" she asked.

"No," I said.

"Have you thought any more about going back to the meetings?" she asked.

"No," I said. See, Mom didn't get it. This moment didn't get a silver lining.

I was sick of stupid AA meetings. For the past two years, I had been in and out of the rooms, crashing one for a few months, then disappearing to drink for a while, then finding another place where I could be a newcomer again. (Getting sober might be hell, but it did give me the world's best underground tour of New York churches.)

I would arrive five minutes late and leave five minutes early, so I could avoid the part where everyone held hands. I thought death lasers were going to shoot out of my fingers if I heard one more person tell me how great sobriety was. Sobriety sucked the biggest donkey dong in the world. One day, a guy just lost it during his share: *I hate this group, and I hate this trap you've put me in, and you're all in a cult, and I hate every minute I spend in here.*

I liked that guy's style.

⌒﹏

WHAT WAS ODD about my aversion to AA was that it had worked for me once before. When I was 25, I ran into a drinking buddy who had gotten sober. I couldn't believe he'd quit. He and

I used to shut down the bars. "One more," we used to say at the end of each pitcher, and we'd "one more" ourselves straight to last call.

But his once-sallow cheeks were rosy. "Come to a meeting with me," he said, and I did.

What I remember best about that first meeting is a jittery reluctance to brand myself with the trademark words. I'd seen the movies, and I knew this was the great, no-backsies moment: *I'm Sarah, and I'm an alcoholic.* For weeks, I'd been kicking the sheets, trying to get square on that issue. What did it *mean* to be an alcoholic? If I said I was one, and I turned out to be wrong— could I change my answer?

Alcoholism is a self-diagnosis. Science offers no biopsy, no home kit to purchase at CVS. Doctors and friends can offer opinions, and you can take a hundred online quizzes. But alcoholism is something you must know in your gut.

I did, even if I was reluctant to let the words pass my lips. I'd read *The Big Book*, AA's essential book of wisdom, and experienced a shock of recognition that felt like being thrown into an electric fence. *Other people cut out brown liquor, too? Other people swear off everything but beer?* Even the way I came into AA was textbook. It was, indeed, the origin story of the group. Bill Wilson spent an evening with a drinking buddy who was clean, and their meeting became the first click of an epiphany. *If that guy can get sober, so can I.* AA had been shrouded in mystery to me, but it can be boiled down to this: two or more drunks in a room, talking to each other.

After that first meeting with my friend, I decided to give it a try. I did not have the most winning attitude. I would sit in the back with my arms crossed and sneer at the stupid slogans. "One day at a time," "Let go and let God," which was clearly missing a verb at the end. I had mental arguments with nearly everyone who spoke. (I usually won.)

It worked anyway. I stayed sober for a year and a half, which is like dog years to a 25-year-old. I heard unforgettable tales in those rooms. I was moved in ways that startled me. Still, I never settled in. A few members took me to brunch one afternoon, all eager hands and church smiles. I sat in that diner—the same diner I used to frequent with my college friends on hangover mornings, when we showed up with cigarette smoke in our clothes and casual sex in our hair—and I hoped to God no one saw me with these middle-age professionals. I shoveled ginger-bread pancakes into my mouth and forced myself to laugh at their jokes, and I worried this would be sobriety: a long series of awkward pancake lunches with people who made me feel old and ordinary. I preferred feeling young and superior.

When I decided to start drinking again at 27, nothing could have convinced me to stay. No persuasive case could have been launched to keep me out of the churning ocean once I decided to swim in it again. For a woman who has hope, logic is the flimsiest foe. Yes, I had admitted I was an alcoholic, and I knew in my heart I didn't drink like other people. I also thought: If I play my cards right, I could get ten more years. *Ten more years of drinking is a long time!*

As more time passed, I began to wonder if I'd overreacted with that whole AA business. This is one of the most common strains of alcoholic doublethink, and it is especially pernicious, because there is no objective way to sort out which person actu-ally *did* overreact and which person is crotch deep in denial. I was the latter, but I was also 27. I spied a window of opportunity and zip-bam-boom. I was headed into the waves once more.

"I'll probably be back one day," I told my friend, but I'm not sure I meant it, because ten years almost did pass, and then I was like: Screw that.

Screw that. For years, this was my attitude toward AA, the place that reached out its hand to me when I was on my knees. But becoming a professional drunk demands you distance yourself from the girl in the foldout chair who was once soul sick and shivering. I never spoke ill of AA after I left. But I could only recommend the solution to someone else. Like telling my friend to cut out dairy while shoving a fistful of cheddar cheese in my mouth.

During that next decade of drinking, I gravitated toward any book or magazine article about a person who drank too much. Nothing pleased me like tales of decadence. I read Caroline Knapp's *Drinking: A Love Story* three times, with tears dripping down my cheeks and a glass of white wine in my hand. White wine was Knapp's nectar of choice, which she described with such eloquence I needed to join her, and I would think, "Yes, yes, she gets it." Then she quit and joined AA, and it was like: *Come on. Isn't there another way?*

Another way. I know there is now, because I have heard so many stories. People who quit on their own. People who find other solutions. I needed to try that, too. I needed to exhaust other possibilities—health regimens, moderation management, the self-help of David Foster Wallace and my Netflix queue—because I needed to be thoroughly convinced I could not do this on my own.

By the way, the guy who got me into AA started drinking again not long after I did. He got married and had a kid. His mid-20s revelry didn't drag into his middle age, which sometimes happens. If you look at the demographics, drinking falls off a cliff after people have children. They can't keep up. "You wanna curb your drinking?" a female friend asked. "Have a baby."

I held on to those words into my mid-30s. I knew some speed bump of circumstance would come along and force me to change. I would get married, and *then* I would quit. I would have a baby, and *then* I would quit. But every opportunity to alter my habits—every challenging job, every financial squeeze— became a reason to drink more, not less. And I knew parenthood didn't stop everyone. The drinking migrated. From bars into living rooms, bathrooms, an empty garage. The drinking was crammed into the hours between a child going down to bed and a mother passing out. I was starting to suspect kids wouldn't stop me. Nothing had.

And I was *so pissed* about that. It wasn't fair that my once-alcoholic friend could reboot his life to include the occasional Miller Lite while he cooked on the grill, and I had broken blood vessels around my eyes from vomiting in the morning. It wasn't fair that my friends could stay at Captain Morgan's pirate ship party while I was drop-kicked into a basement with homeless people chanting the Serenity Prayer. The cri de coeur of sheltered children everywhere: It isn't fair! (Interestingly, I never cursed the world's unfairness back when I was talking my way out of another ticket. People on the winning team rarely notice the game is rigged.)

Three weeks into this sobriety, though, I finally went back to the meetings. I found one near my West Village apartment where they dimmed the lights, and I resumed my old posture: arms crossed, sneer on my face. I went to get my mother off my back. I went to check some box on an invisible list of Things You Must Do. I went to prove to everyone what I strongly suspected: AA would not work for me.

Please understand. I knew AA worked miracles. What nobody ever tells you is that miracles can be very, very uncomfortable.

Work was a respite during that first month, although that's like saying being slapped is a respite from being punched. What I mean is I didn't obsess about alcohol when I was at my job. I didn't tell anyone I'd quit, either, probably for the same reason pregnant women wait three months before announcing their baby. Nobody wants to walk that shit back.

Our office in Midtown became a demilitarized zone for me. What was I going to do, drink at my desk? There was nothing festive about that place. In the depth of the recession, we had moved from an airy loft with brushed-steel fixtures to a bleak cubicle farm with gray carpets and dirty windows. A tube sock sagged the end of an aluminum slat on the Venetian blinds, a bizarre artifact from the previous tenants, and we were all so demoralized and overloaded that it was months before anyone thought to simply reach out and pull the thing down.

The work kept my hyperactive brain buckled in for a spell, though. A friend described her editing job as being pelted to death by pebbles, and when I think back to that summer, all I see are rocks flying at my face—contributors whose checks were late, writers growing antsy for edits. I spent half of the workday combing ridiculous stock pictures to illustrate stories. *Woman with head in her hands. Woman staring out rainy window. Woman tearing out hair.* A montage of the personal essays I was running, and also my life.

Around noon, I'd reach out to my deputy editor Thomas. "Lunch?" I'd type.

He'd type back, "Give me a sec."

"This is bullshit," I'd type with mock impatience. "You are so fucking fired right now. FUCKING FIRED, DO YOU HEAR ME?"

"Ready," he'd type back.

We'd walk to a chain restaurant in the ground floor of the Empire State Building, where I ate a burrito as big as a football, and Thomas calmly explained to me why I was not going to quit my job that day.

Sober folk have a phrase for people who quit drinking and float about with happiness. *In the pink cloud.* I was the opposite of that. I was in a black cloud. A storm cloud. Each day brought new misery into focus. New York: When did it get so unbearable? People: Why do they suck so bad? Sometimes, when I was riding the subway, I would think about burying a hatchet in a stranger's skull. Nothing personal, but: What would it feel like? Would their head sink in like a pumpkin, or would I have to really yawp and swing the hatchet to get it in?

I was not great company, and so I retreated into my apartment. I turned down dinner parties. I excused myself from work events. I listened to podcast interviews, the texture of conversation without the emotional risk. The voices of Terry Gross and Marc Maron filled my apartment so often my neighbors must have thought they were my best friends. And I guess, during those lonely months, they were.

I visited my chic, unsmiling hairstylist in Greenpoint to get my hair done. Nothing like an old-fashioned makeover to turn that grumpy black rain cloud to blue skies. I sat down in her vinyl swivel chair, across from a giant full-length mirror, and was startled by my own reflection: dumpy and sweaty, my chunky thighs spread even wider by the seat. I looked so buried. And as she snipped and measured around my shoulders, all I could think was: *I want to rip off my own face.*

When she was done, she handed me a mirror to see myself from multiple angles. "It looks amazing," I told her. I wanted to die.

No, I did not want to die. I wanted to fast-forward through this dull segment. I want to skip to the part when I was no longer broken and busted up. Was that day coming? Could we skip this part and get there soon? I'd spent years losing time, nights gone in a finger snap, but now I found myself with way too much time. I needed to catapult into a sunnier future, or I needed to slink back to a familiar past, but what I could not bear was the slow and aching present. Much of my life has been this way. A complete inability to tolerate the moment.

But the moments were adding up. Day 32. Day 35. Day 41.

One small gift was that I did not crave cigarettes. I detested the smell, and even the thought of smoking made me nauseated. It made no sense. I smoked for more than two decades, sometimes two packs a night, but without the booze in my system to build up the nicotine craving, I couldn't have cared less. And yet I would have clawed up the walls to get a six-pack of Sierra Nevada. In case anyone needed a reminder that addiction is complex and variable, there it is. What we long for, what our bodies crave, is as individual as the whorls of our thumb.

I was reminded of this in the AA rooms. One day this guy said, "I just can't believe I'll never do blow off a hooker's ass again." He wasn't being funny. His face was in total despair. I felt terrible for that guy, because it was the same heartbreak I experienced every time I passed a craft cocktail bar or read about the local-beer renaissance. *Paradise lost, motherfucker.*

Each Sunday evening, I walked out to the Hudson River, and I sat on whatever bench was unoccupied by families or nuzzling couples, and I stared across the glistening water at New Jersey. This was crazy to me—a whole other state visible from where

I sat—and I tried to imagine what came after the fast-forward. My future fantasies were not unique. The boyfriend with brown eyes and shaggy hair, the writing award, the lather of love and admiration. But what occurred to me as I sat on the bench was that the fantasies all had one thing in common. I was someone else in them.

What a poignant commentary on my own self-worth—I recast myself in my own daydreams. I wondered what it would take to change this. If I could ever collapse the space between my imaginary self and the human being sitting on the bench. Was it even possible? Because you can be a lot of things in this world, but you can never be another person. That's the deal. You're stuck with yourself.

⁓

I STARTED GOING to a meeting in my neighborhood every morning at 7:30. That was a dicey hour for the girl who struggled to get to work at 10 am, but it was a good alternative to hiding in the closet. I liked the location of that meeting, which was a big airy room inside a pretty church, with a chandelier and a door in back that opened onto a leafy courtyard. I got there at exactly 7:30 am to avoid itchy small talk. Otherwise, people would descend on me in the coffee room, and they would say things like, "How are you doing today?" and it was like: *Jesus, stop prying.*

The meetings weren't bad. I liked listening to stories about people's last gasps. Overdoses, alcohol poisoning, swerving down roads in a blackout. There were riveting narratives, but it was also astonishing what the human body could endure. And I couldn't believe how articulate people were. As I listened to them share some epic tragedy or riff on some philosophical point, I wondered: *Where is this speech coming from? Are they reading from a teleprompter?*

I struggled to string words together. I always assumed people who quit drinking snap into shape. But often they fall apart, which was certainly what happened to me. I was experiencing classic signs of withdrawal. The hammering heart, the slow response time, the sensation of moving underwater. But I didn't understand it at the time. I just knew I felt sluggish and stupid. I wanted to be strong and forceful again.

On the 15-minute walk to the church each morning, I started scripting out what I was going to say in the meeting. I wanted people to know I was intelligent and well spoken like they were; I didn't want to remain silent and unknowable. I buffed and polished my revelations, rehearsing them in my mind: *I used to think drinking made me more interesting, but then I realized it made* other *people more interesting.* I liked to insert a twist when I shared, a surprise ending of sorts. Personal essays work on this principle of inverted expectations. A writer friend described the arc like this: *Let me tell you why it's all their fault. Now let me tell you why it's really mine.*

I took my seat in that pretty room, and I spent the first 30 minutes practicing my script and the second 30 minutes scouring the room for my next boyfriend. You're not supposed to do this, but I did it anyway. Fuck you, I was there at 7:30 am, and I could do whatever I wanted. I had been single for nearly three years—the better part of a presidential term. I'd never been around so many lonely, haunted men in broad daylight. Any halfway decent one was a candidate for my future spouse. I listened to the guys share their inner turmoil, and I leaned toward them in my seat, already coming to terms with their deficiencies. *I could date a bald man. Forty-five isn't that old.* But then he would gesture to show the glint of a wedding ring or mention the girlfriend back home, and I'd sink back into my chair, defeated.

One morning, a guy I'd never seen before showed up to tell his story. He was thin and lanky, with a five o'clock shadow, a leather jacket, and boots. He had acne scars on his face, like the bad guy in *Grease*, but he had the eloquence of a natural-born speaker. What struck me were not the details of his story but how he told it. He inhabited his own body. He never raised his voice, but he pulled me toward him with each word dropped into a room of anticipation. I stopped looking at the clock. The chaos in my brain was replaced by a tight spotlight containing nothing but him.

On the subway ride to work, I could not let go of that guy. I wondered how he felt about living on a farm in upstate New York. We could commute into the city during the week, spend weekends reading books in bed to each other with nothing in the background but the chirping outside. We should probably date first. There was a new upscale comfort food place I'd been meaning to try.

I realized I was moving fast, but I also knew—*I knew*—that I was destined to find a boyfriend in those rooms, and I was not saying it *had* to be this guy, but there were several qualities to recommend him. He was sober, for one thing. He did not have a wedding ring, for another. *I could love a man with scars on his face. I would not be embarrassed by his leather jacket and his boots.* And he probably didn't even realize how verbally gifted he was. I had so much to teach him.

I promised myself I would talk to him should he ever come back. *Really enjoyed your story. Wanted to chat with you more about that thing.* A week later, he did come back. Like we were in a romantic comedy, he came back! And my heart did a triple lutz to find him across from me. The meeting that morning was a round-robin discussion, and he was at four o'clock and I was at 7, and when it was his turn, he offered the same effortless poetry I'd heard earlier. Except this time he talked about his boyfriend.

Wait: His boyfriend? He was gay? The focus on the lens sharpened, and I could see it clearly now. *Of course he was gay.* Everyone could see that, except the chubby little lonely heart sitting at seven o'clock, drawing sparkly rainbows on the page with her glitter crayon. I was still beating myself up when the round-robin arrived to me, and I sputtered along trying to assemble some phony epiphany with strong verbs, but tears dripped down my face.

The room fell into silence as people waited for me to explain. But what could I possibly say? That I had just discovered my future husband was gay? That I was going to live the rest of my days surrounded by nothing but empty lasagna pans and an overloved cat destined to die before me?

"I'm sorry," I finally said. "I was just reminded of something very painful." And I guess that wasn't a lie.

<hr/>

IN AUGUST, ALMOST 60 days after I stopped drinking, Anna went into labor back in Texas. This was the best news in ages. I kept my phone with me at all times, even taking it to the bathroom.

In our early 20s, Anna and I had a pact. If one of us got pregnant (and there were a few scares), we'd move in together and raise the kid. We'd both become mothers at once. I understood Anna had a different partner now, and I would not be required to throw my fate in with hers. But I still wanted to be available, because I had been unavailable for so long, dominating our phone conversations with my own self-pity.

I heard the double beep in the early afternoon, and the news popped up on my screen. *Alice. Seven pounds. Healthy.* And I typed back on my phone, "See? I knew it was a boy!"

During her pregnancy, Anna and I had a playful banter about

the gender of her child, which she refused to find out beforehand, and I wanted to make her laugh. I've never been satisfied with being like other people, throwing yet another "congratulations!" on the pile.

But she didn't respond. I kept checking the phone, waiting for the news of her laughter. After a few hours of not hearing back, though, I began to question my strategy. Maybe that joke wasn't so funny. Maybe jokes were better suited for less momentous occasions, ones that didn't involve IV drips and hospital beds and squalling newborns covered in goo. That evening, my phone did not beep. It did not beep many, many times.

The next day at work, I became so consumed by remorse I couldn't concentrate. I dragged Thomas to lunch, and I explained the whole saga.

"She's probably very busy with the baby," he said. Thomas was not quite indulging in this crisis as much as I'd hoped. "I'm sure it's fine," he said, although he winced slightly when he said it, which meant the joke might have been more wrongheaded than I'd feared. I tried out the story on three more people. They all told me it was no big deal, and I was pretty sure they were all lying.

I grew panicky. Was it possible to crater 15 years of friendship with one poorly timed text? I suspected I was overreacting, even as I spun out, but I had spent so many years apologizing for things I did not remember that I had lost faith in my own goodness. Every pocket of silence felt like fingers pointed at me. Certain newly sober people will swallow the world's blame. Everything ever done must be their fault. Just add it to their bill.

I sent Anna an overnight care package, a collection of pop-up books for Alice. *The Hungry Caterpillar. The Little Prince. The House on Pooh Corner.* A few days later, though, I decided this was not enough. I compiled another box of gifts, kitschier this time.

Apparently I wanted to be the first person in history to win back my best friend with a CD containing lullaby versions of Bon Jovi hits.

I was obsessed with my tiny failure. Why hadn't I just said: *I'm happy for you. I'm here for you. Congratulations.* Would that be so hard? What was wrong with me?

For years, I'd hated myself for drinking, but I didn't expect to hate myself this much after I quit. My self-loathing was like a bone I couldn't stop gnawing. Pretty soon, it morphed into anger at Anna. Didn't she understand what I was going through? How could she cut me out like this? Such an opera of despair. No wonder I drank, I thought. It made my own self-created drama disappear.

About a week after the delivery, Anna finally called. I was reading in bed one lazy Saturday with Bubba curled up alongside me when I saw her name on the phone. My breath hitched as if the call were from a long-lost boyfriend.

"I'm sorry I haven't called you before now," she said. Her voice was soft. She sounded exhausted and maybe a bit scared. But I heard a tenderness, too, and it assured me the long, cracked desert I'd just crawled across was a punishment that existed entirely in my mind. "Do you have a minute?"

"Yeah," I said, sitting up. "I have about a thousand."

It was one of those fragile moments when I didn't want to move, for fear any sudden commotion might cause one of us to flutter away. But I also had a desire to escape the pain cave of my apartment and walk in the open air. As we spoke, I tippy-toed down the creaky stairs and made my way along the quietest of the tree-lined avenues to the benches along the Hudson, where I could sit and stare at New Jersey and feel the sun on my shoulders before it slipped behind the horizon once more.

We talked for a long time. She told me how painful and frightening that delivery was. How glorious and uncertain the first days of motherhood were. So much she didn't know. She watched people she barely knew cradle a child she had created but had not yet learned to hold. I didn't tell her about the explosion of anguish set off by my dumb text message. I didn't mention the text message at all. I tried to be a good friend, and just listen.

But I worried that I was waking up to my own life just in time to watch people slip away. The word "recovery" suggests you are getting something back. How come the only thing I felt was loss?

I wanted to apologize to Anna. Dealing with myself honestly for the first time was starting to make me realize what she'd been shouldering all these years. The hours absorbing my catalog of misery, gluing me together only to watch me bust apart. But how many times can you apologize to one person? I was also reluctant to make this another conversation about me. She was moving into a new phase of life—marked by worry, fear, fatigue—and I stood there, mute and blinking, stranded in the mistakes of my own past.

I wanted the gift of forgetting. Boozy love songs and broken-hearted ballads know the torture of remembering. *If drinking don't kill me, her memory will*, George Jones sang, and I got it. The blackouts were horrible. It was hideous to let those nights slide into a crack in the ground. But even scarier was to take responsibility for the mess I'd made. Even scarier was to remember your own life.

⌒

DRINKERS AND FORMER drinkers have this in common: They seek each other out in the night. In the loneliest hours, I often reached out to writers I knew had quit. Emails intended to look casual, like I wasn't asking for help, but what I really wanted to know was: How did you do it? How can I do what you did?

Strange currents lead us to each other. Back when I was in

my late 20s, a guy typed into the search bar "I fucking drink too much," and it brought him to a post where I'd written those exact words, and I was so proud. Through the magic of the Internet, and Google search function, and my WordPress blog—his little message in a bottle found my shore.

Whenever I wrote my own random emails to other people, I was often awed by the attentiveness of their responses. These people barely knew me. We live in an age when most of us can't be bothered to capitalize emails or spell out the words "are" and "you," and yet, these letters were often expansive, full of honesty and care. Maybe it's easier to be our best selves with strangers. People we'll never know long enough to let down.

Often they said: *I was like you once. I used to think that program was bullshit, too.* And hearing they were wrong made me suspect I was wrong, too.

AA was a humble program. A program of suggestions, never rules. It was a place of storytelling, which operated on the same principle as great literature: Through your story, I hear my own.

I was also beginning to realize that getting sober wasn't some giant leap into sunlight. It was a series of small steps in the same direction. You say "I'll do this today," and then you say the same thing the next day, and you keep going, one foot in front of the other, until you make it out of the woods.

I can't believe I'd once thought the only interesting part of a story was when the heroine was drinking. Because those can be some of the most mind-numbing stories in the world. Is there any more obnoxious hero than a dead-eyed drunk, repeating herself? I was stuck in those reruns for years—the same conversations, the same humiliations, the same remorse, and there's no narrative tension there, believe me. It was one big cycle of Same Old Shit.

Sobriety wasn't the boring part. Sobriety was the plot twist.

⌒

EIGHT

EXTREMELY UNCOMFORTABLE
FOR THE GROUP

My friend Charlotte met me for lunch on a sparkling day in fall.

"So you're not drinking," Charlotte said. "How's that going?"

A fair question. It was, perhaps, the only question I cared about. But I could not take the emotional splatter paint in my chest and translate it into words for her benefit. What could I possibly say? That I could sense every drinker in the room, and I hated every one of them? Drinkers had started to throb from every patio and sidewalk. A few days before, I'd gotten a whiff of a drunk homeless guy in the subway and my mouth watered. *Like a vampire.*

"Good," I told her, and stared at the floor for a long time, which is always superconvincing.

Charlotte is my friend Stephanie's younger sister. As teenagers, we met on back porches with domestic beer in our hands and shared the frustration of standing in Stephanie's shadow. As adults, we met at smoking windows with purple mouths to complain about the ways the world still placed us second. She was one of my best friends in New York. We used to share rooms on girls' weekends—two days of binge drinking and sisterly bonding—and I would go home feeling so understood, my stomach sore from laughing.

Now we sat at the table with nothing but awkwardness and salted butter between us. My glass of Perrier was such flimsy compensation—all the fizz of champagne and none of its deliverance.

Why couldn't I tell Charlotte the truth that I was miserable without drinking? Isn't that what friends provide—a soft landing for your complicated pain?

But I relied on the alcohol to loosen my tongue. *Actually,* I would say, leaning in after the second glass, *I'm a wreck.*

I'm a wreck, too! the woman would say, because every female was hoarding some secret misery.

I couldn't achieve such pliability at noon on a Saturday, though. And I didn't want to bore Charlotte with lame stories of 12-step meetings and day counts. (One of the many downsides of my snarky attitude toward "recovery people" was the mortifying discovery I was *one of them.*) I felt sorry for Charlotte, confined to sit across from such a wretch. Sobriety could be so isolating. Sometimes I felt like I was living on an island, where all I did was hope a friend would float by, and when they finally arrived, I began to wonder when they'd go away.

I was a fire starter once. I could talk to anyone when I was drinking. I played therapist, devil's advocate, clown. I actually used to brag I could be friends with Stalin. And it never occurred to me to ask: *Who the hell would want to be friends with Stalin?*

But the woman who threw open her arms to despots had become the woman who couldn't meet the eyes of an old friend.

I felt judged and evaluated by Charlotte. Not because of anything she said, or any look she'd given me, but because judging
and evaluating is what the old me would have done in her place.

I used to hate it when a friend wasn't drinking. *Good for
you!* I'd say, but inside, I was steaming. Drinking was a shared
activity, and one person's abstinence was a violation of protocol.
I measured a friend's loyalty by her ability to stay by my side.
Could she go another round? Would she take a shot for me? My
friends didn't necessarily drink as much as I did, but they were
often the women who stuck around till the lights came up. We
remained in the foxhole as long as our comrades needed us.

Lisa and I used to joke that we couldn't leave the bar till at
least one of us cried. What were we crying about? It's hard to
say. We were both editors, and we got tired and worn down. Our
napkins would be smudgy with mascara by last call, and I'd pat
her on the back as we left. *I think we did some good work today.*

A few months after I quit drinking, I went out with Lisa, and
she *didn't even order a beer.* I hated that my sobriety had become
her punishment.

My therapist didn't understand my objection. "Is it possible
Lisa *likes* supporting you?"

Maybe. But the arrangement didn't seem right. I had a lot of
vegetarian friends, and none of them took away my bacon.

I think some part of me felt guilty for quitting. Drinking was
central to our connections. A necessary prop of companionship
and commiseration. As a friend, I considered myself clutch. Forever willing to split a bottle (or three) and play midwife to your
sorrows.

But my drinking had not brought me closer to these women.
In fact, the opposite happened. The last time Charlotte and I
drank together, I met her and some friends at a nice restaurant.

I arrived late, and the waitress was slow to bring my wineglass, so I grabbed the bottle from the middle of the table and took a slug. My dress was on inside out. ("I got dressed in the dark," I explained to Charlotte, though I neglected to add, *after three margaritas*.) At a bar later, we started talking about female orgasms, and nobody was listening to me, so I kept having to yell. Charlotte gave me $20 for the cab ride home, and I wrote her an email the next day to thank her profusely. It took her two days to respond, which was probably my first sign she was choosing her words.

I love you so much, she wrote me. *But sometimes when you are drinking you act irrationally. You were a little hostile on Friday, and it was extremely uncomfortable for the group.*

My eyes skipped over the parts where she said how great I was and stuck on the other words instead. *Hostile. Extremely uncomfortable. For the group.*

Women are so careful with each other's feelings. We know the world shoots poison daggers into our egos—and we shoot them into ourselves—and so we rush to each other's sides for triage: *Yes, you were fine last night; yes, you are perfect exactly as you are.* (Classic *Onion* headline: *Female Friends Spend Raucous Night Validating the Living Shit Out of Each Other.*) We become such reliable yes-women that any negative feedback is viewed as a betrayal, and the only place we feel comfortable being honest is behind each other's back. *Did you hear what she said last night? Did you see what she wore?* These are the paths of least resistance—the unswerving praise, the gossip dressed up as maternal concern—and it can be very tricky to break rank and say, out loud, to each other: No, you weren't fine at all.

There is no good way to confront a friend who is drinking too much, although doing it when you're not drunk is a good start. Anything you say will cause pain, because a woman who is drinking too much becomes terrified other people will notice. Every time I got an email like the one Charlotte sent, I felt like I'd been trailing toilet paper from my jeans. For, like, ten years. I also burned with anger, because I didn't like the fact that my closest friends had been murmuring behind cupped hands about me, and I told myself that if they loved me, they wouldn't care about this stuff. But that's the opposite of how friendships work. When someone loves you, they care enormously.

Now I was four months sober—in part because of exchanges like the one with Charlotte. I made this lunch date with her, in part to prove how together I was. I hadn't seen her since the night I grabbed the wine off the table in front of her friends, and I wanted to replace the unseemly memory with a better one.

"I'm sorry I'm not very interesting," I told her. *I'm sorry.* Two words I said so often I wanted to hire a skywriter to emblazon the blue horizon with my regret. *I'm sorry for everything.* After lunch, I walked Charlotte to the subway, and we hugged for a long time, and neither of us knew what to say, so we said nothing.

Some recovering alcoholics believe you need to distance yourself from your old friends. They're triggers and bad influences. But what if your friends were the ones who saved you? Who closed out your bar tab and texted with you until you made it home safely? What if your friends were the ones who noticed when you disappeared, who rummaged around their own insides until they could find a compassionate way to say: *Enough?* Was I supposed to cut them out now? When I needed them more than ever?

A FEW MONTHS later, I walked out of Whole Foods holding heavy paper bags only to discover it was sprinkling. I spent

30 minutes trying to hail a cab, and when I picked up the bags, their bottoms had turned soggy and started sagging out. The absurd contortions required to carry those suckers into a cab and up four flights of stairs to my teensy-tiny apartment was a tragedy of errors that left me demoralized and wondering, once again: *Why the hell am I living in New York?*

I'd been debating the question for years. The city was too expensive. Cold, crowded, miserable. Then again, maybe the city was the greatest on earth, and *I* was the one who was miserable. For a long time, my unhappiness was a smear in which offending colors were hard to tease out. What was the source of my sadness, and what was its collateral damage? Removing one element from my life—alcohol—rendered my problems into black and white. The city may have been the greatest on earth, but it didn't feel like me. Not the new me, anyway. I was ready to move back to Texas.

My sponsor cautioned me to wait a year, because people who quit drinking are desperate to parachute out of difficult feelings. Alcoholics are escape artists and dopamine fiends. They will dive into strenuous exercise, wanton sex, obsessive hobbies, impulsive moves across the country to live with people they've just met. The only thing I was diving into in those days was work and red velvet cupcakes. But I took my sponsor's advice anyway and waited a year. My long exile in relapse-land made me question my own good judgment.

For a long time I didn't understand the role of a sponsor. I thought of her like a teacher keeping an invisible score sheet. "You should raise your hand more in the meetings," she told me, and I nodded, and then I never did it. This was how I often operated. I said yes to please you, and then I did whatever I wanted. I thought of it as "being nice." Now I think of it as "being manipulative."

I apologized when I "forgot" to call her or when a suggestion she made "slipped my mind." But I was starting to realize this routine was bankrupt. This routine got me here.

My sponsor pushed me to be honest. Don't make excuses. If I didn't want to talk in the meetings, tell her why. If I didn't feel like calling her that day, admit as much. This approach made me tense. What was I supposed to say? "Hey, it's Sarah. I didn't call you yesterday because I didn't want to call you." But my sponsor said, sure, I could tell her that. It would be a great start. The point was: Own your own feelings, skepticism, irrational rage. Stop pretending to be someone you aren't, because otherwise you have to go into hiding whenever you can't keep up the act.

I didn't think of myself as someone who didn't own her own feelings. I had a few years when feelings were about the only things I *did* own, along with three Hefty bags of clothes, deodorant, and the sound track to *Xanadu*. I was all feeling, baby. Pour that Grenache down my throat and the emotion oozed out like vanilla soft-serve. But there's a difference between blurting out every feeling you've ever had and simply acknowledging the relevant ones. I had two speeds, which often varied with my blood-alcohol level: fine with whatever, and never, ever satisfied. Where was the balance between these?

Although I was incredibly good at having feelings—inflaming them with drink and torch songs—I was incredibly lousy at doing anything about them. I kept flashing back to an argument I used to have with my ex. Every time I vented about work, he rushed to handcraft a solution, which was an irritating habit. *All you want to do is* fix *me*, I spat at him once. But I never thought to ask—Why do I have such a high tolerance for being broken?

OK, so: solutions. In late May, I gave notice at my job. My boss was quite generous about this. He asked if I wanted to work part-time from Texas, an offer I eventually took him up on, but on the day I gave notice, I only felt relief. Freedom. All those days of swallowing the urge to leave, and I finally got the satisfaction of coughing it up.

That afternoon, I left our drab office and walked into the weird no-man's-land of the Garment District. I texted Anna. "Holy shit. I just quit my job!" I was standing in front of a strange window display made entirely of old-timey hats. I walked back and forth, jacked on adrenaline as I awaited her response. I paced a long time. No response ever came.

Didn't she understand I was taking a victory lap right now and she was being very chintzy with her garlands? I knew her job was draining. She helped run a legal aid office in West Texas, and anyone in the business of saving the world can tell you it requires a rather long to-do list. But this had never been a problem before. Why had everything changed, the moment I needed everything to go back?

I went to a meeting, and instead of performing rehearsed lines, I spoke in a flood. "It's like my best friend abandoned me," I said. "I understand that she's a new mother"—and when I said these words, an older woman in the front row let out a guffaw, which left me very confused. It's humbling not to understand your own punch line.

Anna called that weekend. "I feel terrible I didn't text you back," she said. She had a work crisis and responding slipped her mind. And the longer the hang time, the more she raised the bar for herself on the response, which is how three days passed.

I understood. But I also understood our friendship had become another obligation to her, instead of a reprieve. And because I was holed up on my sad little island, it did not occur to me that she might be on a sad little island, too. Or that the

entire world was full of people on sad little islands: people struggling with their children, people struggling just to have children, people desperate to get married, people desperate to get
divorced. Like me, Anna was forging a new identity. "You don't
want to hear about boring mother stuff," she told me. And actually, I did, but maybe she meant she didn't want to talk about it.

I began packing up my things and shipping them back to
Texas in installments. I painted the walls of my apartment back
to their original white. I binged on Marc Maron interviews, five
or six in a row, which were like instructional tapes on how to talk
to people. Maron had been sober for years. He was open about
himself, and in return, his guests would open up about themselves. The discussions that unfolded were riveting, evidence
that two people, anywhere, can find common ground. I liked
reminding myself what an honest conversation sounded like.

That's what I wanted. An honest conversation. Not one where
my mouth turned into a geyser of random confessions—my bra
fits funny, and I once boned that bartender—but a conversation
in which those superficial details faded away and we dared to
tell the truth about our own suffering. This was the closeness I
had always been drinking toward. I drank for other reasons, so
many other reasons, but closeness was the richest reward. The
part where we locked in on each other, and one person sifted out
the contradictions of who they were and how they got there, and
the other person just . . . listened.

I'm not sure when I stopped listening. Somehow it became my
duty to entertain the masses. To be *always on*. I stopped being
someone who talked *with* their friends and I started talking *at*
them. Amusing anecdotes, rants deployed on cue. I wasn't the
only one. We were all out there on our social media stages with
clever quips and jazz hands. This was not a cultural moment

that rewarded quiet contemplation. A colleague once described our media job like this: "News happened. Are you pro or con?" Not "News happened—and should we discuss it?" But pick a side. She who judges first wins the Google searches.

Heavy drinkers are also dreadful listeners, because they are consumed with their next fix. They nod, and smile, but an inquisition is unfolding inside. *How much booze is left? Would anyone care if I got another round? What time does the liquor store close?*

I was trying to stay quiet for a while. Watching, reading, observing. I forgot what an introvert I could be. I had drowned that shy little girl in so many 12-packs that whenever she emerged, nervous and twitching, I was nearly choked with shame. But long before I became an attention hog who yelled about orgasms, I was a child terrified the teacher would call on me, and I needed to accept both extremes in myself so I might find some middle ground. "I think we are well-advised to keep on nodding terms with the people we used to be," Joan Didion wrote. "Otherwise they turn up unannounced."

A week before I moved back to Texas, Stephanie and I had dinner. I hadn't seen her much. She'd spent most of the year in Los Angeles, where her husband was filming a television show and where she was auditioning for roles she didn't get, and didn't tell me about, because it was easier that way.

She asked me how I'd been, and I said scared. I asked how she'd been, and she said lonely.

After dinner, we walked through the quaint West Village streets where I came each weekend to shake loose my solitude. She'd had a few hard years, and I hadn't even noticed it. How is it possible to be good friends with a person and miss so much? But Stephanie had such early career success that, in my mind, it could only continue. Yes, being an actress over 35 was rough, and yes, rejection sucked, but she was Stephanie. My forever dream girl. Everything always worked out for her.

If you scratch the surface on anyone's life, you find ache and pain. I don't care who they are. They can be the Queen of England. (Especially if they are the Queen of England.) I'd been so busy envying Stephanie, trying to compete with her glow, that I stopped *seeing* her. I didn't notice the times she reached out for me. "I need you back," she once told me after too many saketinis, and I thought: *Wait. Where the hell did I go?*

More than a year had passed since that night. After dinner, I brought her to the bench looking out across the water to New Jersey, and she sat beside me, and we didn't say much.

"I could not have made it in this city without you," I said. She waved my words away before the tears had any chance. Stephanie doesn't like these speeches. "Stop it. We'll be just as close," she said, and she was right.

The next week, a year to the day I got sober, I moved back to Dallas, the city where Stephanie and I once sat in a chain restaurant, promising each other we would escape to New York.

I found a crooked little carriage house, with leafy trees all around, where I made French press coffee, just like Stephanie made when I first visited her in New York. I hung the Japanese robe I first saw her wear, and I bought aviator sunglasses like the ones she had. And I smiled at all the many ways she has shown me what I hope to be in this world.

⌒⌒

RIGHT BEFORE MOVING, I sent out an "I'm coming back!" email to my friends in Dallas. The premise was to ask if anyone had housing tips, but the real intent was to drum up enthusiasm about my return. I waited for the exclamation marks and all-caps emails to fill my in-box. A handful of people responded. Otherwise, I was greeted by the sound of wind whistling through an empty canyon.

"It's not like I expected a parade," I told my mom, which was another way of saying: I was totally expecting a parade, and this blows.

I worried I had screwed up by choosing to return to Dallas. I always figured I'd wind up in Austin, weird and wacky Austin, except every time I visited that town I had a nagging suspicion too many people loved it, and every time I visited Dallas, I had a nagging feeling not enough did.

Dallas had evolved from the place I grew up. More walkable areas and cool coffee shops, fewer cement slabs and soulless redevelopment. I think some part of me wanted to reckon with my past. I grew up in Dallas, so embarrassed for the person I was. Maybe I needed to assure that little girl: Hey, kid, this place isn't so bad.

I also longed to be close to my family again. My parents had moved out of the ritzy school district and bought a modest and lovely house near the lake, with my mother's grand piano in the bay window and a backyard filled with shade trees and a handsome dog that didn't obey. A wisteria vine grew outside the guest bedroom window. My favorite flower, planted where any weary visitor might see it each morning. My brother had moved back to Dallas after living all over the globe—London, Italy, Iraq—and he launched a full-scale campaign to get me home. He whipped out his wallet: What will it take to get you back?

Most of us need to push away from our families at some point, and there's nothing wrong with that. But there's also nothing wrong with wanting them close again. Many people choose alternate families in sobriety. I chose my real one instead.

WHEN I LIVED in Dallas in my late 20s, my ass was hot-glued to a bar stool. The thing I knew best about my hometown was the drink specials. Now I faced a question that would greet me in any city in the country: What did people *do*, anyway?

On Friday nights, I loaded up on craft projects. Needlepoint. A latch-hook rug of a tabby. A cross-stitch of the cast from *The Breakfast Club*. I was one butter sculpture shy of a state fair submission, and I didn't care. My hands needed occupation. I needed to do something—instead of sitting around, thinking about the one thing I didn't get.

When you quit drinking, you are sandbagged by the way alcohol is threaded into our social structure. Drinking is the center of weddings, holidays, birthdays, office parties, funerals, lavish trips to exotic locales. But drinking is also the center of every-day life. "Let's get a drink," we say to each other, when what we mean is "Let's spend time together." It's almost as if, in absence of alcohol, we have no idea what to do. "Let's take a walk in the park" would be met with some very confused glances.

My old Dallas gang was a group of salty male colleagues who gathered at the bar after work. Not *a* bar, mind you, but *the* bar. "The bar" was a complete sentence. It was both a question and a command. (The bar? The bar. The bar!) I had missed those guys, and I flattered myself they might miss me, too.

"I'd love to hang out sometime," I emailed one of the guys.

"Totally," he responded. "You know where to find us."

Well, shit. I suppose it was wrong to be hurt by this indifference to the script I'd written in my mind—the one where he and I went to lunch and talked about real things that mattered.

Once upon a time, we'd gathered around that long wooden

table and gulped down whatever was being served. We laughed and drank while the sun sank in the sky, and I got a high being the lone female in the foamy man cave. Those guys were all married, but that didn't matter (to me, at least), and I never quite knew whether we were flirting, or not flirting, and I told myself both stories, as suited my needs.

I wondered if I threatened them now that I was sober. The first person to stop drinking in any group can cast a pall—like the first couple to get divorced, or the first person to lose a parent. I also wondered if they threatened *me* now. I watched their Facebook feeds a bit too carefully, judging them for every babbling 2 am status update, every picture of a whiskey glass hoisted into the lens. How dare they stay on Pleasure Island after I had moved away. I wondered: *How long could they possibly keep this up?* One of them had just won the National Magazine award for profile writing, so apparently the answer was: As long as they wanted.

It took a long time to accept that other people's drinking was not my business. It took a long time to admit I'm the one who left the bar, not the other way around. You can't move away for six years and come home to find all the furniture in the same place. Those guys had different lives now. New kids, new jobs. Two of them were divorced and dating 25-year-olds, which must have taken up a great deal of texting time.

Sobriety has a way of sorting out your friendships. They begin to fall into two categories: people you feel comfortable being yourself with—and everyone else.

Allison was in the former category. We had met years ago on a garden patio in Brooklyn, where we got drunk and declared ourselves great friends. But months went by between visits. Some friendships are like that. They lack an escape velocity.

She lived in Dallas now, and we met one night at a Mexican

restaurant. She didn't drink much anymore, a quality I was starting to value in a person. She also looked looser, freer than the striving girl I'd met in New York.

"I love it here," she said, and I kept waiting for her to circle back and revise that statement. Tell me the real truth. But that was the real truth. She was happy.

"When was the last time we saw each other?" I asked her as we scanned the menu. And then I smacked the table like it was a buzzer. "I know. Your thirty-sixth birthday party."

"You're right!" she said. "Oh my God. Do you remember that night?"

Dammit. How many more times was I going to get torpedoed by this question? It's like I needed a fill-in-the-blank letter of apology.

Dear _____, I'm so sorry I _____ all those years ago. You must have felt very _____ when I _____. I drank too much _____ that night, and was not in my right mind.

"Actually, I don't," I said.

"You fell down my staircase," she said.

I covered my face with my hands and peeked at her through the slats of my fingers. "Yeah, I used to do that."

"My stairs were *marble*," she said. "It was terrifying. Honestly, I'd never seen anything like it. You don't remember this at all?"

No, but I remembered how I woke up the next morning, and I thought: *How did that awesome party end? Maybe I should send Allison a text. "Had a great time last night! The part I can remember was amazing!"*

But I didn't send anything like that. In fact, I stopped talking to Allison for two years.

The psychology of the blackout drinker is one of dodge and denial. Things you can't remember become epic in your mind. Five minutes of unremembered conversation can be a shame you carry through the rest of your life. Or it can be shrugged off entirely. I did both, and the problem was that you ended up cutting people out without even knowing why. You got a hunch that something bad happened, so—snip, snip. Easier that way.

"I thought you hated me," Allison said, and I was confused. Why would *I* hate *her*?

She wasn't entirely off base, though. Not that I hated her, but I avoided her, the same way I avoided every pesky truth that threatened my good times in those days. I spent so much time spinning imaginary stories in my own mind—what might have happened, how I needed to repair it—and very little time finding out what I had done.

Over the next years, I would have more honest conversations like this, in which patient friends with understanding faces filled in parts of my story I didn't recall. No, you didn't do anything weird that night. Or yes, you were a disaster. Whatever the revelation, it was never as painful as the years of worry that lead up to it. Usually, we ended those discussions much closer.

That's what happened with Allison and me. When we said good-bye that night, we talked about getting together the next week. And this time, we followed through.

⁓

MY CHILDHOOD BEST friend Jennifer got sober one year after I did. This shocked me. I never thought she had a drinking problem. But when I looked back on the nights we spent together in our late 20s and early 30s, the signs were there. Chronic unhappiness. Chaotic life. Mysterious fender benders.

She used to carry a picture of her husband in her car, back before they got married, and she would stare at his face before walking into any party. She had a problem with drunken flirtation and needed to remind herself: *This is the man you love. Don't mess it up.* But after building this tiny obstacle of resistance, she'd walk into the party and wash it away again.

After having two kids, she became one of those moms who kept a bottle of red wine forever handy. The minivan was not going to change her. Her party plan worked for a while, but then the wheels started coming off. Her blackouts became so frequent that when she was drinking, she would only communicate via text, so she could have an evidence trail of her decisions.

She and I had always been control freaks. Yet we both drank to the point of losing control. It sounds contradictory, but it makes total sense. The demands of perfectionism are exhausting, and it's hard to live with a tyrant. Especially the one in your own mind.

So she quit drinking, and we found ourselves, once again, two lonely members of an outsider tribe. We began taking long walks around the lake, sharing all the stories we had not told in the years of superficial catch-up. We stayed up talking at her house, and some nights it was like we were 13 years old again, laughing so hard we almost peed, except instead of her mom telling us to keep it down we were interrupted by her daughter, dragging a fuzzy blanket. "I can't sleep," she would say, finger in mouth, and she would hop up into her mother's lap, one last stint in the world's safest place.

Talking was the glue of our world, never drinking. We were good talkers. Our conversations were so natural, so obvious. She would talk, and then I would talk, and then somehow, through this simple back-and-forth, we could start to hear the sound of our own voices.

NINE

BINGE

One afternoon, I got an urge to pull into the drive-through at Jack in the Box. Do I like Jack in the Box? Not particularly. But the urge snagged me, and before I could unsnag myself, I was on the conveyor belt that led to the drive-through's metal box, where I ordered my carb explosion. What I noticed—as I idled there with a queasy feeling like I was getting away with something—was that absolutely no one was going to stop me. The bored teenager wearing a headset did not ask "Are you sure about this, ma'am?" The woman who swiped my credit card did not raise an eyebrow, because she had seen so much worse. There were precious few barricades between my stupid, fleeting impulse and the moment I sat on the floor of my living room with ketchup covering my fingers and chin.

"I just ate an Ultimate Cheeseburger," I told my friend Mary. She lived around the corner from me, and she had been a champion binge eater most of her life.

"Oh, honey," she said. "Did you get the curly fries, too?"

"I can't believe you even asked that."

"I'm sorry, sweetie. Of course you did."

When addiction lives in you, it sprouts many vines. For the first year after I quit drinking, I refused to worry about food. I would do whatever it took to give up alcohol, which included a typical dependency swap: Trade booze for smokes. Or trade smokes for Double Stuf Oreos. Or Nutella. Or Double Stuf Oreos with Nutella.

A year and a half of drinking nothing should've made me proud. But a year and a half of eating everything in my path had left me defeated and ashamed.

"I think I need to go on a diet," I told Mary, lobbing the words into the air before I could snatch them back. Diet: the toxic buzzword of body dysmorphia. Diet: those things destined to fail.

In the old days, a heroine in search of happiness lost weight and found a prince. But current wisdom dictates a heroine in search of happiness should ditch the prince, skip the diet—and gain acceptance. Stop changing yourself to please the world and start finding happiness within. That's a good message, given all the ways women are knocked around by the beauty-industrial complex.

But my problem wasn't a deficit of acceptance. It was too much. I drank however I wanted, and I accepted the nights that slipped away from me. I ate however I wanted, and I accepted my body was a home I'd never want to claim as my own. Sitting on that linoleum floor, surrounded by empty foil wrappers and my own disgust, I wondered if I could use a little less acceptance around here. Or, to be more precise: Acceptance was only half the equation. The other half was determining what was unacceptable—and changing that.

I DON'T KNOW when I stopped taking care of myself. In college, Anna used to foist vegetables on me, which was exactly what my mother used to do when I was a child. They were both healthy eaters, who saw beauty in nature's bounty, and I was a hedonist who liked slapping away her broccoli. I had the tastes of a frat boy, or a grumpy toddler. No to vegetables. Yes to ranch dressing. I actually described the food I liked as "nothing healthy."

My brother is defiant like this, too, which suggests either a genetic predisposition to Ultimate Cheeseburgers or a rebellion against the bean sprouts and barley of our food co-op childhood. Kids often dive into the indulgences their parents place off-limits: television, sugar, sex. And I became an adult who actually enjoyed carpet bombing her gut with processed meats. "The next time you eat a fast-food burger, I want you to really *think* about it," a friend once said. So I did. And I thought: This is great!

Of course, I had the added pressure of growing up female in the diet culture of the '80s. After the age of 12, food stopped being sustenance and turned into guilt, sin, reward, penance, entertainment, love. Cramming food into my mouth brought a rush of rebellion, but I was never sure who I was fighting. My mother? The advertising industry? Jane Fonda? (Poor Jane Fonda. She was only trying to help.) Whoever I intended to punish with that routine, the only one who got hurt in the end was me.

Our bodies carry the evidence of our neglect. By the time I stopped drinking, I was nearly 50 pounds overweight. I had ulcers that felt like the lit end of a cigarette held up to my stomach lining. I had a mysterious rash splashed over my arms and legs. I had two twisted knees that cried out when I descended stairs, a painful reminder I literally could not support my own weight.

I never thought of myself as neglectful. I'd been a single woman living in New York City, after all. I took care of myself *all the time*. I opened tightly sealed jars by myself, banging a spoon against the metal until it relented, and I installed shelves in my kitchen, using a power drill and torpedo level to hang them properly. I couldn't fob off the finances to my spreadsheet-oriented husband. My wife never did the laundry. (Actually, the women at the drop-off dry cleaner did my laundry, and I thank them.) I carried the responsibility of rent and work demands on my own tensed shoulders, and the way I eased those knots was to reward myself with a nice bottle of wine at the end of a long day. Maybe a six-pack as well. *This* was taking care of myself: a conscious decision not to shame myself for my own roaring appetites.

Go to any spa, and you'll see the same philosophy at play. *It's time to take care of you finally—here's a glass of champagne.* When it comes to selling the luxury experience, alcohol is more central than warm hand towels and tinkling water sculptures. They serve booze at beauty salons, high-end stores, resorts, upscale hotels. What's the most famous perk of flying first class? Free drinks, of course. Alcohol is the ultimate in pampering.

But "pampering myself" all the time led to a certain sloth. I let cat food tins languish in corners, and I let bills go unpaid. In Brooklyn, I was sleeping with a guy who used to come over at 3 am, and in between tokes on his one-hitter one night, he said, "Baby, you need a new couch." I looked closer and was startled by what I saw: My velvety red futon had become filthy with splotches of soy sauce and red wine. There was a strange crust on one cushion that might have been cheese. It's not a good sign when your stoned fuck buddy is giving you decorating tips.

People who don't take care of themselves will also struggle to take care of others. One night, I came home so blind drunk I left the front door flapping open, and at some point, my cat walked out into the night right before my eyes. *My cat.* The one I was beyond paranoid about keeping indoors. The one I loved with such ferocity I thought I might go insane if anything happened to him. The next morning, I was in a panic trying to find him, only to open the front door and see him sitting on the stoop, looking up like: *Where have you been?*

I couldn't believe I let that happen. But addiction siphons so much attention, and the most precious treasures will get tossed in the backseat: children, husbands, basic hygiene. I heard a guy once complain about how much he wet the bed when he was drunk. But he didn't stop drinking. He got waterproof sheets.

And I get it. When you are alone and drinking every night till you pass out, who really cares?

I asked myself that often. *Who really cares?* I'd given up many things by the end. Hanging my clothes. Making the bed. Shaving my legs. Zippers or clothing with structure of any kind. I threw towels over spills until the towels began to seem like rugs.

And I told myself this was OK, because our society was beyond warped in its expectations of women, who were tsunamied by messages of self-improvement, from teeth whiteners to self-tanners. I was exhausted by the switchbacks of fashion, in which everyone was straightening their hair one year and embracing their natural curls the next. I wanted to kick the whole world in the nuts and live the rest of my years in sweatpants that smelled vaguely like salami, because *who really cares?*

It took a while for me to realize: *I cared.* I didn't need to do these things because it pleased men, or because it was what I was "supposed" to do, or because my mother clipped something out for me from O magazine. I should take care of myself because it made *me* happy. Remarkably, impossibly—it felt good.

~

FOUR MONTHS AFTER moving to Dallas, I went on a diet. It was one of those old-fashioned diets with frozen fish sticks in geometric shapes, a serious throwback in the day of lemon-juice fasts and lap bands. I walked out of the strip-mall store where I had weekly weigh-ins with all the shame of a pastor emerging from an adult video store at 1 pm.

Why was I so embarrassed? Because I felt like a failure to both sides of the body wars. To women for whom appearance was everything, I was a source of pity. To women for whom diets were evil, I was a sellout.

When I was coming into my teen years, diets were nearly a developmental stage. Adolescence, motherhood, diet, death. But by the time I walked into that fluorescent office, covered in pictures of women in smart suits with their arms raised overhead, the word "diet" had become radioactive—thanks in part to female writers I knew and admired, who fought against the false notion that thin was synonymous with health. The past ten years had seen the media embrace more curves and cushioning, all of which signaled progress—but none of which meant I needed 50 extra pounds.

Still, I worried I was letting my anti-diet friends down—as though my intensely personal body choices needed to be their choices, too. The whole point of feminism was that we deserved the agency of our own choices—pro-choice, in the truest sense of the term—and yet I feared my friends would judge me as frivolous, or vain. But fearing another person's opinion never stops them from having one. And my focus on external judgment kept me from noticing the endless ways I'd judged myself.

For the past decade, I did that horrible thing, resolving not to think about my weight and yet thinking about it constantly. Every time I awoke. Every time I passed reflective glass. Every time I saw an old friend and I watched their eyes go up and down me. At some point, no one complimented me on anything but my hair and my handbags. I was certainly vain then; I just didn't happen to look like someone who should have been.

Mine was a recipe for unhappiness. I was fixated on my weight but unwilling to do anything about it. And I couldn't do anything about it while I was drinking, because booze left me roughly 1,200 calories in the hole four times a week. There's not a miracle diet in the world that can pull you out of that quicksand. In fact, when I did try to diet, I made a mess. Cutting out carbs and swapping beer for liquor is a trusty formula for blacking out.

So I went the old-school route. Calorie restriction. Reasonable portions. Water, not diet soda. Half the steak, not the whole steak consumed and instantly regretted with a sigh and one hand on my belly. After a lifetime of "all or nothing," I needed to learn "some."

The weight fell off me. Fifty pounds in six months, as if it never wanted to be there. I was astonished by the lack of trauma this entailed, after all those years of bad-mouthing diets as a form of punishment and deprivation. And the scale couldn't tell the whole story of my change. I woke up, and I felt happy.

I stopped avoiding cameras and old friends. My underwire bra no longer dug into my belly, which was a constant source of grump. When I passed a mirror, I was startled by the person I'd become. Although perhaps it was more accurate to say: I was startled by the person I could've been all along. The person I had buried.

Self-destruction is a taste I've savored much of my life. The scratch in my throat left by too much smoking, the jitteriness of a third cup of coffee, the perverse thrill of knowing a thing is bad and choosing it anyway—these are all familiar kinks, and one feeds the other. But was it possible to change my palate— to crave something good for me, to create an inspiration spiral instead of a shame spiral?

I started making my bed each morning, even though I was going to climb in it later at night. I started washing the dishes in the evenings, because I liked waking up in a clean house. I started going to yoga, which is an entire practice of learning to support your own body.

"You're stronger than you realize," my pink-haired yoga instructor told me one day, as I wobbled my way through a handstand, and I started thinking she might be right.

I turned on physical exercise a long time ago. I was a kid who loved the slap of dirt on her hands, but middle school gym was a reminder of my early puberty and late-round draft pick status. I withdrew indoors, into films and books and fizzy bottles. I hissed at organized sports and hid from any activity that broke a sweat, and what I mostly thought about my body is that I wished I didn't have one. I preferred virtual realms. Email, phone, Internet. To this day, I love writing in bed, covered in blankets. Like I'm nothing but a head and typing fingers.

So I started inhabiting my own body again, because it was

not going to go away. I rode my sea-foam green bike along the wide tree-lined avenues of my neighborhood. I took long walks, in which my mind dangled like a kite string.

People noticed when I lost weight. *You look so healthy. You look so great.* And as much as I enjoyed these compliments, I feared them as well: that they would go away, or that I was too greedy for them in the first place. It made me uncomfortable how much my weight loss changed my perceived value. After I quit drinking, I saw the world differently. But after I lost weight, the world saw *me* differently.

It was like I'd suddenly become visible, after years of camouflage I didn't know I was wearing. There is something undeniably attractive about a person who is not hiding—in clothes, under extra weight, behind her addictions. My mother and Anna were right all along: There was great beauty in nature.

⌘

IN THE EVENINGS, I pulled out a leash for Bubba so we could walk outside in the buzzing summer night. The cat had been sick for a while. He was 15 years old. I didn't know how much longer he had, and if I wasn't careful, I could spend a whole day freaking out about this.

When I met Bubba, he was an outdoor cat. But one day he came back to my ex-boyfriend's apartment with incisor bites in the side of his cheek, like two toothpicks through raw dough. There was a series of expensive surgeries. A long stretch of recovery time. He became an indoor cat after that.

It was a miserable power struggle to break him. I don't know if you've ever tried to win an argument with a cat, but good luck with that. He would slip out when we weren't looking, settle scores in some back alley near midnight, and return two days later like Don Draper crashing through the front door after a bender. *What? What are you looking at?*

I loved him for all of this. I, too, was drawn to places that would destroy me. I, too, came home with bruises, and it never stopped me. The cat was an appealing mix of strapping adventurer and cuddle bug. People say cats are aloof, but they are just very, very discerning about whom they trust. I liked caring for that cranky little guy. Women can be very good at ladling their love into the unsmiling mouth of a creature who nonetheless needs them.

I come from a long line of nurses on both sides of my family. We give gentle strokes and change bedpans and wipe up vomit splashed on the floor while cracking vaguely inappropriate jokes. When I think about my own failure to take care of myself, I wonder sometimes if I wasn't unconsciously waiting for someone like me to come along. Pay off my credit cards, clean up my oopsies. Other people's messes can be so much more interesting than our own.

Maybe that's why I needed the cat so much. This may sound absurd, but cats are caretakers. They will kill your mice and curl up at your side when you're ill. One night in Brooklyn, I became fluish and had to lie on the cold tile floor of the bathroom with my pillow and a duvet. It was one of those moments when my loneliness ached like a broken bone. And the cat padded into the bathroom and lay down beside me, and we slept like this, both of us curled against the warm side of the other.

Now it was my turn to take care of him. The sickness required pills, popped into his mouth twice a day. X-rays, constant experimentation with his food. Jennifer was a veterinarian now; the child who once saved wounded birds had grown up to be a woman who saved people's pets. When Bubba got sick, she was the person we both needed.

My new house was mere blocks from where Bubba had once prowled, and when he started meowing at the door again—after years of remaining silent on the issue—I wanted to do something for him. Let him roam his home turf again, before he died. I wanted to find some compromise where he could venture into the lusty outdoors that called to him—but stay tethered to me.

The leash was my big idea. Jennifer swore up and down it wouldn't work. Leashes were against a cat's nature, she insisted, and for a long time, she was right. Then one day, I put on his harness—blue vinyl ropes along his haunches, like he was about to jump out of an airplane—and he discovered this simple act of surrender led to the outside world.

He inched through the doorway with his nose twitching. When his paws touched the familiar dirt, his whole body went electric. This. All of this. The breeze in his fur. Those feral smells. A blade of grass dragged along the side of his mouth. He rolled around in the dirt. He sniffed the grille of my car like it contained all the decadence of the world.

He tugged too hard, then I tugged too hard, but eventually we found our rhythm. We got so good at this nightly routine, we could stay out there for an hour at a time, exploring grassy corners and wandering into the undiscovered country of the driveway. He lay with his fur against the cool gravel, and I stared up at the sky, two animals finding their way into the wild on a short leash now.

〜〜〜

TEN

SEX

My first date in sobriety was with a guy I knew from college. When I saw him at the restaurant, he was more attractive than I remembered, though he was wearing jeans that either marked him as above fashion or distressingly behind it.

"I don't mind if you drink," I lied to him.

"I know," he said, and ordered a Coke.

I was getting to the place where I needed to date. (Not *want*, mind you, but need.) In the cocoon of my crooked little carriage house, I watched documentaries back to back and unspooled fantasy lives with men I'd never met. The tattooed waiter who read Michael Chabon. The handyman with Paul Newman eyes. I could see myself losing years this way, living nowhere but between my ears.

So I forced myself out the front door with trembling hands and burgundy lip gloss. All dating is an unknown country, but as far as I knew, mine was uninhabitable. Even friends who didn't struggle with raging booze problems were unclear how I was going to date without alcohol. "I don't think I've ever kissed a guy for the first time without drinking," said my 27-year-old coworker Tracy. And she was a *professional sex writer*.

How did this happen? We were worldly twenty-first-century women, who listened to sex podcasts and shared tips on vibrators and knew all the naughty peepholes of the Internet. And yet somehow we acquired all this advanced knowledge of sex—threesomes, BDSM, anal—and zero mastery over its most basic building block. The idea of kissing unmoored me. Touching a man's lips to mine without the numbing agent of a three-beer buzz sounded like picking up a downed wire and placing it in my mouth.

After dinner, my old college friend took me to a coffee shop, where I drank hot chocolate on a breezy patio. I liked him. (Mostly.) He was a doctor. He remembered the oddest details about me from college, which was flattering, like he'd been thinking about me all along. I told him a poignant story about my past, because I sensed this was the scooching-closer portion of the evening, and he took my hand, which was resting on the table. Such a simple gesture: four fingers slipped into the crook of my own. But with that subtle and natural movement, my arm became encased in a block of ice. *Oh God, the panic.* I was afraid to pull away. I was afraid to invite him closer. I was like a doe who had spied the red laser sighting of a gun on my chest. *Do not move.*

They say drinking arrests your emotional development at the age when you start using it to bypass discomfort, and nothing reminded me of that like sex. In the year and a half since I'd quit, I had confronted so many early and unformed parts of myself, but sex continued to make me downright squeamish. I was horrified by the vulnerability it entailed. Sometimes I walked around in disbelief about blow jobs. Not that I'd given them, but that anyone had, ever.

As I sat on the patio with my frozen robot arm, I kept flashing to an alternate version of this date. The one where I poured rocket fuel down my throat and went barreling toward him with a parted mouth. Instead, when he dropped me off, I darted from his front seat so fast I practically left a cloud of dust. *Thankyounicetoseeyougoodnight.* I climbed into my bed and pulled the duvet up to my chin, and I understood that I was probably never going to have sex again. Because if you only know one road into town, and the road collapses, what can you do?

Alcohol was the beginning of sex. It was there the first time I kissed a guy, at the age of 13. It was there the last time I slept with a guy I'd only just met, two months before getting sober—a bartender at Lisa's fortieth birthday party who spoke just enough English to convince me to leave with him. In the nearly quarter century that spanned those two points, alcohol let me be and act however I wanted. One of my favorite ways to have sex was right before a blackout, when I was still there but I'd gone feral, and I could let all those low and dirty words spill out of my mouth. *Do this. Do that.* But now I wasn't sure if I liked sex that way because it felt good or because guys dug it when I got wild. That's what I wanted more than my own pleasure. To make myself irresistible. To blow his freaking mind.

I was worried men wouldn't like dating a sober woman. After all, drinking was a part of our erotic social contract. It was a long-standing agreement that we would all drink away our nervousness and better judgment. I'd heard about men who got frustrated when their dates weren't drinking. "How am I going to take advantage of you now?" one guy asked my friend, which was a joke, but a lot of uncomfortable truth was beneath the punch line. Alcohol is the greatest seduction tool ever invented, and to order a seltzer with lime is to take that shining scimitar out of a man's hand and toss it in the nearby Dumpster.

I went to dinner again with the doctor. I was torn about him. He made me laugh. He was a great listener. But he cussed out some dude who cut him off in traffic. He told this overinvolved story about his ex and described her with various synonyms for "psycho." The jeans: Was it shallow that I cared? That old pendulum swung in my mind the entire evening. *I'm going to kiss him / Oh hell no, I'm not.* I couldn't tell if the tics that bothered me about him were red flags or convenient excuses to stay in my hidey-hole. I'd lost touch with my own gut instinct.

And I thought: If I could take a shot of Patrón, I could kiss him. If I could suck down the beer (or five) that he does not order on my behalf, then we could do this the way it is done. We could find ourselves wrapped in sheets, clothes in a heap near the foot of the bed, my tricky Grecian top in a tourniquet around my forearm because I was so frantic to rip it off, to be unloosed, to be free. And afterward we could evaluate. Do we work? Is this a thing? We could exchange flirtatious glances over brunch, or we could scatter to other corners of the galaxy and avoid each other in grocery stores. Either one was fine. But at least something would happen.

Something else happened instead. I sent him an email that took way too long to write. *I can't be more than friends with you.* The drawbridge, which for a brief moment lowered, snapped shut again. I was so relieved.

When I said I would never have sex again, that probably sounded dramatic. The kind of grandiose proclamation a teenager makes before slamming the door to her room. It's not as though every intimacy in my entire life had been warped by booze. I'd had quiet sex, and giggling sex, and sex so delicate it was like a soap bubble perched on the tip of my finger. I knew such joy could exist between two people, but I had no clue how to get to it anymore. My only directions involved taking a glass of wine to my lips and letting the sweet release show me the way.

Clearly, I needed a new map.

I KNEW ONLINE dating would come for me someday. It was the fate of all single women in their late 30s to stare down a personal profile, and as far as punishments go, this was fairly benign. Once, my type faced spinsterhood and destitution. Now I had to walk into the gallows of OK Cupid and drum up a good attitude about emoticons.

Online dating was not a bad move for me. It allowed me to inch toward intimacy with built-in distance. It granted me the clarity that "hanging out at the bar" often lacked. One of the great, unheralded aspects of Internet dating was that the word "dating" was in the title, thus eliminating any ambiguity. Were we dating? Was this a date? The answer was yes.

It also allowed me to say up front: *I don't drink.* I'd worried so much about how to reveal this. I didn't want to watch some guy's face fall when I ordered a Diet Coke and then endure the pecks of his curiosity. So my "ABOUT ME" statement began "I used to drink, but I don't anymore." I've had stronger openings, but this one was good for now.

I understood that not drinking—and *not drinking* to such an extent that it was the first detail I shared about myself—would turn off certain guys. I saw them sniffing around my profile. Those bearded eccentrics with their fluency in HBO shows and single-malt Scotch. How I missed those beautiful, damaged men, but we kept our distance from each other. Occasionally I would email one of them, and they never wrote back, and I got it. Back when I was drinking, I wouldn't have responded to me, either.

My first weeks on the site were choppy, but I soon became accustomed to the routine. The endorphin blast of attraction. The coy banter that allowed you to tease out someone's personality. Flirting was like any exercise: It got easier the more you did it.

This wasn't the first time I had tried online dating. About six months after I moved to New York, I signed on to Match.com. I did it for Anna. She'd logged so much time listening to me complain about my ex. "Just try it," she said, which is a very hard argument to win.

I bought a bottle of sauvignon blanc that night and sipped my way onto a plateau of cleverness. I didn't want a profile that was drab and ordinary. I wanted a personal statement that grabbed every guy by the collar and whispered each word into his mouth. I swear I was in love with myself by the time I finished, a bottle having morphed into a six-pack of beer, and I posted the hottest picture of myself I had: a close-up taken by a professional photographer in which I appeared 20 pounds lighter than I was. I woke up the next day to a kitchen clogged with cigarette smoke, and the memory surfaced in pieces: *I think I joined a dating site last night.*

I got several messages on the site that day, but two stood out. One was from a successful businessman with silver hair. The other was from an indie-rock type who frequented a burger shop less than two blocks from my front door. Those two men had nothing in common, but their notes had a similar sincerity. They wanted to meet. This week. Tomorrow. Now.

I called my friend Aaron in a panic. "What do I do?"

He spoke slowly. "You write them back, and maybe you meet them."

"But I can't," I said. Having portrayed myself as the overthinking hedonist's Marilyn Monroe, I could not bear to disappoint them. There was not a pair of Spanx in the world big enough to bridge the distance between the woman on that site and the woman who stood in my kitchen, pacing in jogging pants.

"If you're worried about misrepresenting your weight, there's an easy fix for that," Aaron told me. "Put up a full-body picture of the way you really look."

"You're right, you're right. Of course you're right."

I pulled my profile down the next day.

This story was one of a thousand reminders that dating was never easier when I was drinking. Alcohol may have turned me into Cinderella for a few radiant hours, but I would wake up in dishrags again, crying about the messes I'd made.

This time, the process of finding the right person on the site was more honest, but it was also slow. A lot of dead-end conversations. A lot of dudes in camo posing in front of their giant trucks. I was growing antsy. Some days I thought about finding a random dude and just banging him.

What was wrong with me? Why did I think sex was something I needed to get over with?

❦

MY FIRST ONLINE date was with a divorced father who was an immigration lawyer. He was nice, but not for me. No chemistry. When he offered to make me a lavish meal on Valentine's for our third date, I knew the only proper response was to gently fold up the tent on our time together. He deserved to spend that holiday with someone who felt differently about him. I was starting to learn one of the most important lessons of online dating: the wisdom of saying no.

All my life I fought to say yes. I was shy and ambitious, a terrible mix, and so I tried to dismantle my isolationist tendencies. Yes to this party I don't want to go to, yes to this person I don't want to date, yes to this assignment I'm afraid to botch, because saying yes was the path to a remarkable life. I needed to say yes, because I needed to push myself off the couch and into the swift-moving stream of hurt and jubilation. But saying yes to everything meant repeatedly saying no to my own better judgment, or drinking myself to the point I had none. Now my job was to sort out the possibilities with more caution: which risks are not worth it, and which ones deserve a jump.

I said no to the smart guy who wasn't attractive to me. I said no to the cocky guy who was. I said no to the graphic designer who tried to kiss me one night. Our date was fun. I ran the pool table (twice), and his eyes roamed along my ass as I lined up my shot, and I was surprised to find I liked that. But he slurped down three bourbons in 90 minutes, and when he leaned forward to kiss me, I was grossed out by the sour smell of his breath, the slump of his eyes, and I ducked. Like in a sitcom, I literally ducked.

It was a revelation to me how unappealing men were when they were drunk. Back when I was dating my college boyfriend Patrick, who was sober, he would pull away from me when I was buzzed and handsy. "You smell like a brewery," he'd say, and I didn't get it. I *felt* so sexy in those moments; it only followed I must have *looked* that way. Now I realized what a sadistic game drinking played. It built up your confidence at the very moment you were looking your worst.

After the comical way I ducked the graphic designer's kiss, I was certain I'd never hear from him again. But he texted me the next day. Turns out, I accidentally inflamed his desire. I went out with him again, but something crucial was lacking. "I don't think this is going to work," I told him, which was a phrase I was learning to say. It felt foreign on my tongue.

"I have never broken up with anyone in my life," I used to tell people, as though it marked me as kind, as though it granted me broken-heart status. In truth, it was evidence of my passiveness and my need. I had never ended a relationship, but that was another way of saying I'd never found the courage. I'd let someone else do the dirty work. The dating site was good practice for me. Wind sprints in proper boundary setting.

I went out with a guy named Ben. He showed up in jeans and a '70s ringer shirt pocked with holes and said, "Look, I dressed up for you," and already I liked him. He had brown eyes that caught the light.

We sat in a bar that was delightfully sleazy, and he drank a beer and I drank water, and nothing was forced or uncomfortable about this arrangement, which was shocking in itself. He asked me why I quit drinking, and I told him. I asked why he and his wife split, and he told me. We both baby-stepped toward each other, one refusal to lie at a time. When he walked me to my car, he said, "So I'm unemployed, I'm broke, and I still live with my ex. I understand if you never want to see me again, but you should know all that."

I saw him the next week. What the hell, he was different. We sat outside a gelato store with our feet kicked up on the railing, and we talked about pornography. I can't remember now who opened the door in the conversation leading to the hallway that contained beaver shots, but he told a story about the first dirty picture he ever saw. *Hustler* magazine, the hard-core stuff. All these women spreading their labias, six of them stacked on the page like bricks in a wall, and he felt a little ruined by it. Because after that, he needed so much just to get the same scorpion sting.

He'd gone to college during a wave of antiporn sentiment in the late '80s, and he'd learned to be ashamed of his desires. Then he got married. Then the marriage caved. Now all he wanted was to dig himself out of the rubble and figure out who he was.

I let him kiss me that night. A lovely, soft, and unfrightening kiss. "I'll call you," he said, but he didn't, and that was fine, too, because some relationships are good to say yes to for a very short time. It was nice to learn that rejection didn't have to burn.

I thought about Ben sometimes. I thought about the photo of all the labias, because some part of his description reminded me of the pretty boys I used to cut out of teen magazines and plaster over every inch of my fifth-grade bedroom. Maybe this was my own version of a beaver shot: all those puppy-dog eyes staring at me, boring into me. I wondered why women like me complained about pornography setting up unrealistic expectations for men, but we rarely talked about how romantic comedies—and the entire bubble-blowing industry of teen magazines and obsessive pop songs—set up unrealistic expectations for us, and I wondered if I was a little ruined, too.

Maybe we all were ruined. Porn and Hollywood clichés were like the wooden framework that built dating sites. The women wanted walks on the beach, exotic trips, someone to talk to after a long day at work. The guys claimed to want that, too, and then they would show up in your in-box, demanding a tit shot.

The more I hung around the dating site, the more I suspected a few of those guys could use a little more shame about their desires. I couldn't believe the things men would ask of a woman they'd never met. *I'm in town for a weekend away from my wife. Would you like no-strings-attached sex?* Or: *I really can't meet for coffee, but I am willing to fuck.* And so I practiced saying no, because clearly these guys weren't hearing that word enough.

A 23-year-old sent a flirty message one day, and I wrote back, telling him I was flattered, but he was a little too young for me. "Nonsense," he replied. "Age isn't nothin' but a number. All it means is that I have more to cum in your face."

First of all: He needed to double-check his science. And second of all: No. Noooooooo, young sir, no way in any time or temperate zone. What happened? What warp of etiquette and eroticism had conspired to result in such a blisteringly wrong sentence?

These guys were way too enabled by the false intimacy of the Internet, which allowed you to toss out come-ons you would never utter if you were staring into another person's eyes. The frightening reality of another human being, the frightening reality of our imperfect and stuttering selves. How much technology has been designed to avoid this? We're all looking for ways to be close at a distance. Alcohol bridged the gap for me, the way the Internet bridges the gap for others. But maybe everyone needs to stop trying to leap over these fucking gaps and accept how scary it is to be real and vulnerable in the world.

One night in April, I went out with a guy who was studying psychology. We ate at a fried chicken restaurant, one of those trendy places where they served comfort food that used to be trashy. The guy talked fast, and I enjoyed the thrill of trying to keep up. "You're a contrarian," I told him, licking grease off my fingers.

"Is that good?" he asked. "I want to be the thing that you like." And it was the first time someone had said this to me, but I recognized it as my driving motto for the past 25 years. It was nice to be on the other side for a change.

"It's good," I said. "I like hearing your mind tick."

He intrigued me. We talked about bike lanes and Elvis Costello. For months, I'd been going on dates, wondering if something was wrong with me. Why was it so rare to be attracted to a person who was also attracted to you? But maybe it works this way so when it happens, it feels special. What I felt for the guy that night was unmistakable.

We sat in front of my house in his car, both of us staring forward.

"I don't know what to do next," he said. "I don't know if you want me to kiss you, or..." His words trailed off, and I leaned over and pecked him on his cheek before anything more could happen. I was so unnerved by this newfound chemistry, I dashed out of his car, but I regretted my timidity. Later, in the safety of my own pink bedsheets, I could not stop thinking about him. My body alighted imagining what might have happened if I'd been bolder, if I'd opened up again. What good was caution if you couldn't chunk it into the breeze?

I texted him. "I should have let you kiss me."

The double beep of his response was fast.

A week later, I drove out to his place, and we had dinner, and as we sat on the mattress of his messy bedroom, he turned to me and said, "Do you want to fuck?"

This was my first clue I was not exactly in a Lifetime movie. There would be no soft stroking of my hair. No spray of rose petals across the bed. But in fact, I did want to fuck. I'd gone nearly two years without sex. Two years without drinking, or smoking, or fucking, which was a long spell without the company of your favorite vices. And so I said, "Yes."

If you were hoping my first time in sobriety would be meaningful and tender, or at least hot and exciting, then we were wishing for the same thing. But it was fast, and efficient, and that was OK. Sometimes it's best not to wait for the perfect movie moment; those can leave you checking your watch for a long time.

Afterward, we stared up at the ceiling of his bedroom as though it contained a moon. "I always think of the worst things to say after sex," he said.

I know there is a woman who would have left that invitation alone, but I was not her. "What are you thinking?" I asked.

"I'm thinking: Well, that was free."

It was a joke. (I guess?) Maybe he thought the sex was lousy, and he was joking that at least he didn't pay for it. Or the sex wasn't lousy, but he was joking about what a horrible, self-sabotaging thing that would be to say. Honestly, I didn't understand the joke, so I won't parse it on his behalf, because what I discovered over the next week was that the psychology major had some major psychology issues. He was twisted up like a tornado inside. (Also, he was a dick.) A few days after this incident, we had a conversation in which he displayed such casual cruelty I walked away knowing—possibly for the first time in my life—that it was nothing I did. Some people are so brimful with misery they can't help splashing everyone else.

So there it was, my big chance to get sex right again, and I went and screwed an asshole. Maybe I should have felt crestfallen, but I didn't. I chalked it up to a learning curve. It was fine. I never saw him again, and no one was worse for the experience. Actually, I was glad for the experience, because it taught me that good sex wasn't a function of sobriety, any more than good sex was a function of being drunk. Good sex was about the person you were with and, maybe more important, the person you could be while you were with them.

⁓

I STARTED SEEING a musician. He was gone too much of the time, and it was never going to work, but I wanted to try. When we sat together, he made me feel light-headed. When he looked at me, I had the giddy feeling of a three-beer buzz.

"You have these drunken, dreamy eyes right now," he told me, and I could feel it, too. Bliss. Until I got sober, I never understood the phrase "weak in the knees." I thought it was an old-timey cliché that women like my mother used. Then my knees spaghettied underneath me as he walked toward me once, and I realized: *Oh my God, this actually happens.*

The first time he and I had sex, I barely remembered it. The whole afternoon was white light and the dance of tree shadows through the windows. He kissed me on the couch, and then he kissed me on the stairs, and then I took him to my bed. And then time stopped.

In the years that followed, I would have more sex like this. Sex that felt good and right. And I noticed when I was with a person I felt comfortable with, I could walk across the room without smothering myself in a blanket. I could let myself be seen. And I noticed when I stopped worrying so much about how I looked, I could lose myself more in how I felt.

I always thought good sex without alcohol would be sharp with detail, saturated with color, but instead it was more like a 4 pm sun flare. Pleasure shuts down the recorder in the brain. The flood of serotonin and dopamine creates a white-hot burst of ecstasy. For decades, I drank myself to reach that place of oblivion. Why hadn't I known? The oblivion could come to me.

⟡

ONE AFTERNOON, JENNIFER showed up at my front gate, holding a Fuji cassette that was dated in her small, careful script: August 23, 1988.

"I can't believe you still have this," I told her.

She smiled. "It's yours now."

I knew what was on the tape. It was a story I didn't like. One that explained a lot about my mixed-up history with drinking, men, and sex. I recorded it two days shy of my fourteenth birthday, when I sat in Jennifer's bedroom with a jambox on my lap, sharing details that would haunt me for decades.

"It probably won't even work anymore," I said, as Jennifer slotted the tape in the deck of an old creaky jambox, once so familiar to us and now quaint as an abacus. She pressed rewind, and the tape chugged backward violently, like an unsteady aircraft preparing to take off.

She pressed the play button, and there was a buzz, followed by a loud clunk. And then, my voice floating back to me from more than a quarter century ago.

"Hi. I'm over at Jennifer's house. It's August 20-something or the other." I do not sound two days away from being 14. My voice sounds more like 17. *"There's really not much to say here. I can't wait for my birthday. I got a sweater."*

On the tape, Jennifer says something from across the room I can't quite make out. It sounds like, *"Tell our friends about your summer."*

"It was the best summer of my life," I start. *"I went down to visit my cousin in Michigan. I met this guy named Brad. He was wonderful. A wonderful person."*

Brad was a sweet stoner type with feathered blond hair and a nod that was about two beats slower than everyone else's. He was 18. The night I met him, he said, "So you're Kimberley's older cousin," and I laughed and corrected him. *Younger.* For weeks, whenever I ran into him, he would pantomime picking his jaw off the floor. "No *way* you're 13," he would say.

I'd smile, blush. Yup, really 13. One afternoon, he kissed me in Kimberley's room, and I couldn't believe it: He had picked *me*. It was everything the movies had promised.

My last night in town was not. We went to a party, had a few drinks, and things got much more confusing.

The story that follows is one I've thought about countless times over the years. I've wrestled with its meaning, rewrote its nuance, tried to erase it from memory. But this was the first time in 25 years I'd sat down and listened to myself tell it:

> We were in this vacant apartment. There was no furniture whatsoever. There were chairs. A beanbag. Foldout chairs. We went into this bedroom. I forgot to close the door. I thought we were just going to talk for a while, but the first thing he did when we got in the room was to take my shirt off. He got down on the floor to take his shoes off, and I guess he noticed the door was open, and I thought he was going to leave. And I was like, Oh my god, what did I do? Do my feet stink? [Jennifer laughs]
>
> So he closes the door, and I go, "Oh I'm sorry," and he goes, "Oh it's no problem." He took off his shoes. I don't know how my pants came off. I never figured it out. I was on the ground somehow. I don't know how I got there, either. He took my underpants off, and he took his underpants off. He was on top of me, and he was trying to do it, but it just hurt so much. It was like a bowling ball stuck up your nostrils. I mean, that is the analogy that I have come to be at one with. I mean, it really, really hurt. I started breathing really, really drastically. And I started making noises, and he told me to be quiet. Well, he didn't tell me to be quiet. He said "Shhhh." And I

couldn't exactly be quiet, because when someone's doing that, you don't want to just go, "Oh yes, this is nice, real nice." I mean, he was like, "Shh, be quiet," and I go, "It hurts," and he goes, "I know, I'm sorry," and I'm like, "You don't know. You could never know."

But he wasn't hard enough. I don't know if that's a personal insult to me, or to him, whether he's impotent or not, I don't know. But he wasn't hard enough, so he turned over and I gave him a hand job, and I guess he liked that, and he tried again, but I couldn't. I mean, not that I physically couldn't, but first of all, it hurt, and second of all, he didn't have protection, and I didn't want to get pregnant, and I didn't know if he had AIDS or whatever. I mean, I'm sure he didn't have AIDS. But I didn't want to lose it that early.

So he never came. I mean he never went that deep in, and then he asked me to give him a blow job, and at first I didn't, but he kept asking me, and I thought, poor guy, he's not going to get it tonight, I guess I'll give him some head. So I did, and that was really gross. It gagged me. In a big way. I was like, "Oh, this is real fun."

And then we had to get up and go. I left the room, but I had to come back for my shoes. And when I came back he kissed me, which made me feel good. Because that made me feel like he didn't regret anything. And then I left, and I've never seen him since, or heard about him. This has got to be boring for anyone who is listening, and this tape is almost out.

I could spend a lifetime unwinding what I heard on the tape. From the fact he had trouble getting hard to the part where he told me to be quiet, to the way I couldn't recall key details of how I wound up on the floor.

I'd had three wine coolers before we went into the room, not enough to black out but enough to have a warm buzz. I remember feeling grateful for the drinks, because otherwise my heart might have punched out of my mouth. I remember lying on the floor, his bare shoulder shifting back and forth in my line of vision, and the voice screaming in my brain: *Am I having sex right now?*

The part that kills me is near the end, when he kisses me. *Because that made me feel like he didn't regret anything.* It was all I cared about at 13. That I wouldn't be someone he'd regret.

There are reasons for statutory rape laws. One is that 18-year-olds have very different expectations of dark and empty rooms than 13-year-old girls. But I was the kind of 13-year-old girl who didn't want to be protected. Forget your laws and your conventions. I was ready for the "best summer of my life." And I wanted to seem unfazed by what was happening. I didn't want him to know how utterly inexperienced I was. I wanted to look cool.

My underpants were bloody when I got home. I spent years wondering if I'd lost my virginity, and if I'd consented, just as I would spend years wondering how I ended up in that Paris hotel room, and why I let Johnson stay in mine.

Was it rape? I don't think so, though part of me still doubts my interpretation. I know some people will read it another way. But one of the great powers we have is the ability to give meaning to our own experience. To me, this was a bad and fumbling early sexual episode that has many meanings. But the one that stands out to me is how I quashed my feelings for the sake of someone else's. His pleasure was important, not mine. His regret was important, not mine. It was a pattern I repeated for years. And every time I did, alcohol was there.

⁓

ABOUT THREE YEARS into my sobriety, I was on a plane from DFW to New York. The guy beside me was 23. Rumpled and exhausted from staying up all night. He slumped beside me and flashed the sideways grin of a boy who gets what he wants. "I'm moving to New York," he said. "Have you been before?"

"I have," I said, and left it at that.

He was moving there to be an actor. *Oh baby, you are screwed,* I thought, but I didn't say this. Instead, we talked about leaps of faith. We talked about Denzel, his favorite actor. I tried to prepare him for disappointment, as I'm sure everyone did: Don't make fame the measure of success, I told him; make this move about learning something.

It was an early morning flight, and around us, heads tilted back with eyes closed and mouths open, so we whispered like two kids talking behind the teacher's back. We talked so long that a three-and-a-half-hour plane ride felt like 30 minutes. I noticed all the times he touched my knee.

I was nearly 40, used up in some corners of history, and men my age were often chasing women with luscious rumps and tits that had yet to sag. I wasn't looking for younger guys, but they seemed to find me anyway, and I wondered why. Maybe they sensed I was not interested in commitment yet. Or maybe they liked the grooves of a hand that knew its own strength. I was done trying to be anyone else.

"Do you think the mile-high club really exists?" he asked, raising his eyebrow.

"I hope not," I said. "Fucking in an airplane bathroom sounds terrible."

He wrinkled his nose. "Yeah, you're right."

Our plane landed, but we were not ready to part. It was his first day in New York, and it was only 11 am, which meant we had time to spray paint the town before we parted. I paid for the cab ride to the Ace Hotel in Midtown, a place where musicians and writers often stayed, and I treated him to lunch at the restaurant, full of downtown charm and bustle. "You are giving me one hell of a story," he said, and I smiled, because he was doing the same for me.

We sat on the couch in the lobby, my legs on his lap. We were surrounded by strangers typing on their laptops, headphones on. Did they notice us? What did they see? He fiddled with my hair, which fell across my brow. He traced his fingers around mine as my hand rested on his knee. Have you ever noticed how astonishing it can be, holding hands with a person? Such an everyday thing, such a nothing gesture. But two hands, barely touching each other. It can feel like flying.

He kissed me then. Right in front of all those people. I didn't care. They were too busy with Twitter and Facebook to pay attention. "I want to put down my credit card and take you upstairs right now," he said. I smiled, and ran my fingers over his sweet face, that face that had taken him so far in the world, and I said, "Not this time."

His body fell back in the couch. "So that's it? You're going to leave now?"

I smiled. That's right. I was going to leave now. But I gave him my number, and I told him to text me if he ever needed me, and I walked out to the bustling sidewalk feeling so light.

It's a fine day when you finally figure out the right time to leave the party.

ELEVEN

POWER BALLAD

People who quit drinking become terrified they will lose
their power. They believe booze makes them the people
they want to be. A better mother. A better lover. A better friend.
Alcohol is one hell of a pitchman, and perhaps his greatest lie is
convincing us we need him, even as he tears us apart.

I needed alcohol to write. At least, that's what I believed. I
had no idea how people wrote without alcohol, which is a bit
like wondering how people construct buildings without alcohol
or assemble watches without alcohol. I'm sure it happens all the
time, but I'd never done it.

Years ago, when I worked at the Dallas paper, I used to sit at
the bar with the other writers, and we'd elbow each other out of
the way to reach the punch lines. Writers are often insecure by
nature, but in those hours I felt indomitable. We could disagree
about music, politics, the use of the serial comma, but we never
disagreed about drinking.

Writers drink. It's what we do. The idea made me feel special, as though I got a pass on certain behaviors, as though self-destruction were my birthright. The bar also made me feel like real work was getting done, even if the real work turned out to be arguing the merits of *Saved by the Bell*.

I liked talking about writing much more than actually writing, which is an unspeakably boring and laborious activity, like moving a pile of bricks from one side of the room to the other. Talking about writing was exciting. It was all possibility. *Let's talk about the story at the bar! Kick it around over a few drinks, brainstorm that bad boy.* And in those sinking moments when I realized two hours had passed, and no one had brought up the story we were supposed to fix, I had the perfect antidote in front of me. Another glass of guilt-be-gone.

But booze wasn't merely a collective procrastination tool. It was the tool I took home with me when I needed to sit by myself and get the words out onto the page. Writing is a lonely profession. Nobody wants to walk in darkness alone.

Alcohol was an emancipator of creativity. It silenced my inner critic. It made me bigger and smaller, and my writing required both delusions: to believe everyone would read my work, and to believe no one would. I even loved writing hungover, when I was too exhausted to argue with myself, allowing words to tumble onto the page.

If I ever grew anxious about the empty bottles my work required, I could wrap myself in an enabling legend. *Writers drink.* It's what we do. As long as the work gets done, you can coast on these words for a very long time.

But the dynamic pivoted for me. The drain and the time suck of my habits became too much to tolerate. I was no longer a writer with a drinking problem. I became, as Irish author

Brendan Behan once said, "a drinker with a writing problem." Something had to go, and given how conjoined my writing and drinking were, I figured it had to be both.

Well, actually, I did have a history of writing without alcohol. It was called childhood. Kids are wizards of imagination, and I was one of those youngsters scribbling all day long. Children are not hobbled by an awareness of others or the fear of people's judgment. Children don't have to face professional failure, public disinterest, the criticism of colleagues, lacerating Twitter commentary, the scorn of strangers. They skip through a grassy meadow where every picture they paint is important, every story worth telling, whereas today's online writer traverses an enemy territory where any random dude with a Tumblr account can take you down.

Perhaps I was using alcohol not to spark my creativity but to blunt my sensitivity. I needed someone to hold my hand.

After I quit drinking, I didn't write for six months. I was too fragile. I spent that time editing personal essays for *Salon*. I loved reading stories of other people's lives, extraordinary things happening to ordinary people. One woman met her dream guy only to watch him die of an aneurysm that very day. One woman was trapped under the rubble after the earthquake in Haiti. She was saved, but the other woman in the house wasn't. It was mind-blowing what could unfold in the course of a life.

The stories got me out of myself, but they also stoked my writer's envy, which isn't necessarily bad. Envy can be an arrow that points to the things you want. The more I read those stories, the more I thought: I could do that. That might feel good. I should join them.

The first thing I wrote in sobriety was an essay about quitting drinking. It felt like insurance for a person prone to relapse.

I wanted to be on record. I wanted to double down on public humiliation to keep me from backsliding. The story wasn't easy to write, but it wasn't that hard, either. When I was done, it sounded like me. The me I remembered.

After the piece published, writers I admired responded with kind words and strangers in the comments responded with a warm stream of urine down my leg. But I was starting to realize this online anger wasn't about me. It was a by-product of garden-variety powerlessness. Usually when I reached out to one of those people, they would say similar things. *Oh, I didn't think anyone was listening*—which suggests the true source of their rage.

I kept writing. I began waking up at 6:30 and writing for the first four hours. No procrastinating. No rearranging the furniture. Just wake up and stare down. The work was never easy, but it became *easier*. Less like a geyser I kept waiting to blow and more like a faucet I could turn on and off.

We ascribe such mystery and magic to the creative process, but its essence is quite basic. Moving a pile of bricks from one side of the room to the other requires strength. Time, discipline, patience.

Writers write. That's what we do.

"The idea that creative endeavor and mind-altering substances are entwined is one of the great pop-intellectual myths of our time," Stephen King wrote in his memoir and instruction manual about creativity, *On Writing*. King is one of the many heroes I've had who turned out to be an addict. He was a serious beer binger, who admits he could barely remember writing his novel *Cujo*.

When I read the stories I wrote during my heaviest drinking years, I don't think they're bad. I am a little appalled, though, at how frequently alcohol intrudes. Interviews take place in bars. Entire narratives revolve around drinking. Jokey asides are made about hangovers and blackouts. A beer or a glass of wine sits in the corner of nearly every piece, like some kind of creepy product placement.

A friend of mine is a music teacher, who says pot helped him truly hear music for the first time. "But if you smoke too much pot," he said, "you get that Jamaican high. Everything turns to reggae." Whatever creative growth alcohol and drugs might offer at first, it doesn't last. You stop learning and noticing.

"Try to be one of the people on whom nothing is lost," Henry James wrote. I first heard the quote in an interview with Pete Hamill, author of the 1994 memoir *A Drinking Life*. As an old-school newspaper reporter growing up among the free-clinking bottles of postwar America, Hamill built his identity on booze. But ultimately he quit, because it was bad for business.

It was bad for mine, too. So much was lost on me when I was drinking. What we did last night, what was said. I stopped being an observer and became way too much of a participant. I still introduce myself to people, only to receive the brittle rejoinder of "We've met, like, four times." Memory erodes as we age. Did I really need to be accelerating my decline?

I'm not saying great writers don't drink, because they certainly do, and some part of me will probably always wish I stayed one of them.

I sometimes read stories by women who are using, and they speak in a seductive purr. They have the intoxicating rhythm of a person writing without inhibitions. Those pieces can trigger a toxic envy in me. Maybe I should do drugs, I think. Maybe I should drink again. How come she gets to do that—and I can't?

Mine are childish urges, the gimme-gimme for another kid's

toys. The real problem is that I still fear my own talent is deficient. This isn't merely a problem for writers who drink; it's a problem for drinkers and writers, period. We are cursed by a gnawing fear that whatever we are—it's not good enough.

If I stew in that toxic envy too long, I start to teeter. Those are the days when my eyes can get pulled by a glass of champagne, throwing its confetti into the air, or the klop-klop of a martini being shaken in a metal cup. What a powerful voodoo—to believe brilliance could be sipped or poured.

I read an interview with Toni Morrison once. She came into the literary world during the drug-addled New Journalism era, but she never bought the hype. "I want to feel what I feel," she said. "Even if it's not happiness."

That is true strength. To want what you have, and not what someone else is holding.

⁓

ABOUT THREE YEARS after getting sober, I decided to learn guitar, something I'd been saying I would do for years. My author's bio used to read "Sarah Hepola would like to learn how to play guitar," as if this ability came from Mount Olympus. I bought an acoustic from my friend Mary, and I holed up in my bedroom, and then I figured out why I never did this in all the years of floating on the booze barge. It was incredibly difficult.

Strumming looked easy, but it was awkward and physically unpleasant at first. It took hours to even form the finger strength to make a handful of chords.

"I think something's wrong with my hands," I told my teacher, one of the best guitarists in town. He assured me that no, my hands were fine. Learning guitar was really that hard.

"You don't think my hands are too small?" I asked.

"I teach eight-year-old girls to play guitar," he said. "You're fine."

But I bet eight-year-old girls don't writhe with the humiliation of being a middle-age beginner. I was confronting the same poisonous self-consciousness and perfectionism that had kept me from speaking Spanish when I was in Ecuador, that kept me from dancing in public when I was sober, that kept me locked up all my life. I hated feeling stupid.

"Your problem is that you step up to every plate and expect to hit a grand slam," a friend told me, and I said, "Yes, exactly!" as though I were simply grateful for the diagnosis. Drinking had fueled such impatience and grandiosity in me.

Addiction was the inverse of honest work. It was everything, right now. I drank away nervousness, and I drank away boredom, and I needed to build a new tolerance. Yes to discomfort, yes to frustration, yes to failure, because it meant I was getting stronger. I refused to be the person who only played games she could win.

The first time I played a song in its entirety—"Sweet Child O' Mine" by Guns N' Roses—I felt like I'd punched a hole in the sky. I blew off work that day, shut down my phone. I sat in my bed and played the song over and over again, till my hands were cramped and red-purple grooves ran like railroad tracks across my fingertips.

The feeling was so immaculate I didn't want to taint it with the anxiety of performance. The next week, during our lesson, I kept my instructor talking, hoping I could burn out the entire hour with questions before we got around to playing. About 30 minutes in, he turned to me and said, "OK, let's hear you."

The ache of those words: *Let's hear you.* It put a plum in my throat to be the person who wanted to play but could not bear to play. To want the microphone but to stand in the back. To know there is a book in you but to never find the nerve to wrestle it out. I was so screwed up on the issue of performance. It's like I didn't want anyone to hear me, but I couldn't shut up. Or rather, I wanted *everyone* to hear me, but only in the way I wanted to be heard, which was an impossible wish, because nobody ever followed instructions.

My hands shook when I strummed through the song, but my teacher strummed along with me, like a father with his hand barely holding the bicycle seat. We sang together, sometimes finding the harmony parts, and afterward he said, "You're a natural." He probably said that to everyone, but I liked that he said it to me.

"This is more like a portable karaoke machine for me," I told him, smoothing my hand along the gloss of the dreadnought.

"That's cool," he said.

"I'm not going to be a good guitarist," I told him.

"You never know," he said.

What mattered was that I was doing something I wanted to do instead of merely talking about it. Later, in the safety of my bedroom, my fingers started to find their way. Sometimes I could make chords without even looking at the strings, and I began to develop a kind of faith, a reaching without fear. The afternoon could slip away when I was like this: three hours, gone without looking once at the clock.

I loved being reminded that losing time didn't have to be a nightmare. It could also be a natural high.

IT'S CRAZY I used to think all writers drink. When you quit, you notice how many don't drink anymore, or never did. This is true for every creative field. Throw a stone in Hollywood, and you'll hit a sober person. Rock stars, comics, visual artists—they learn sobriety is the path to longevity. Any tabloid reader knows that walking into certain AA rooms can be like stumbling into a *Vanity Fair* party, which helped kick the fame delusion out of me.

I was a child who worshipped celebrities—Michael Jackson, Whitney Houston, River Phoenix—each of them was a hero to me. I spent way too many of my younger years grasping for whatever fame I could get my fingers around. But in the battle for a better life, fame is a flimsy weapon. Those rooms were not divided into famous people and nonfamous people. Just people who had all reached for the same fix.

Sobriety helped to knock a few false prophets out of me. Alcohol. Other people's approval. Idealized romantic love. So what should I worship now? I didn't care to find the answer, honestly, but the program kept placing one word back in front of me, even after I pushed it away. *God.*

The word made me squirm. Like so many people, I resisted AA, in part, because of the words "higher power." Even the major work-around of a "God of my understanding" was way too much God for me. I was raised around conservative Christians who did not always strike me as charitable. I was puzzled by the demented winner-takes-all spirit of traditional religion: *I go to heaven, and you do not.* College taught me religion was the opium of the masses. God was for weak people who couldn't handle their own lives, and it took me a long time to understand that, actually, I was a weak person who couldn't handle my own life, and I could probably use all the help I could get.

The "higher power" idea came to me in increments. Like sobriety itself, it was not a spectacular, flailing jump but a tentative inching in the same direction. I thought a lot about storytelling. That was a power way bigger than me. When I listened to someone's story, when I met the eyes of a person in pain, I was lifted out of my own sadness, and the connection between us felt like a supernatural force I could not explain. Wasn't that all I needed? A power bigger than me?

I needed to be reminded I was not alone. I needed to be reminded I was not in charge. I needed to be reminded that a human life is infinitesimal, even as its beauty is tremendous. That I am big and small at once.

I worship the actual stars now, the ones above us. Anna lives out in West Texas, where the night sky burns electric, and her back patio is the first place I understood the phrase "a bowl full of stars." The stars tilt around you, and you can feel the curvature of the earth, and I always end up standing on my tippy-toes out there, just to be two inches closer to the rest of the galaxy.

My spiritual life is in its infancy. But the major epiphany was that I needed one. A lot of my friends are atheists. We don't talk much about belief, and I wouldn't presume to know theirs, but I think their stance comes from an intellectual allergy to organized religion, the great wrongs perpetrated in the name of God, the way one book was turned into a tool of violence, greed, and bigotry. I don't blame them. But I wish belief didn't feel like a choice between blind faith and blanket disavowal. I'm a little freaked out by the certainty on either side. No one has an answer sheet to this test. How we got here, what we are doing—it's the greatest blackout there is.

Whether God exists or not, we need him. Humans are born with a God-shaped hole, a yearning, a hunger to be complete. We get to choose how we fill that hole. David Foster Wallace gave a commencement address at Kenyon College, a speech that is a bit like a sermon for people who don't want to go to church:

> In the day-to-day trenches of adult life, there is actually no such thing as atheism. There is no such thing as not worshipping. Everybody worships. The only choice we get is what to worship. And an outstanding reason for choosing some sort of God or spiritual-type thing to worship—be it J.C. or Allah, be it Yahweh or the Wiccan mother-goddess or the Four Noble Truths or some infrangible set of ethical principles—is that pretty much anything else you worship will eat you alive.

I worshipped alcohol, and it consumed me. I worshipped celebrity and the machines of external validation, and it cratered me. To worship another human being is to set yourself up for failure, because humans are, by their nature, flawed. I worshipped David Foster Wallace once. In some ways, I still do. His suicide is another reminder that all the knowledge and talent in the world will not stop your hands from tying the noose that will hang you.

I seek all the sources of comfort I can find. Music. Old friends. Words that leave my fingers before the sun rises. My guitar, strummed in an empty room. The trees as they turn, telling me that I am not a towering redwood but another leaf scraping the ground. I also hit my knees each morning and bow to the mystery of all I don't know, and I say thank you. Does anyone hear me? I don't know. But I do.

TWELVE

THIS IS THE PLACE

A few months before my cat died, he started sleeping in the closet. I would search the house for him and find those green eyes staring back at me from the corner, underneath the jackets and behind the boots. I knew exactly why he'd chosen that spot, the far-back place where harm couldn't reach. One night, I pulled my duvet off the bed and lay down beside him to let him know I would stay at his side. About a minute into this routine, he bolted downstairs and hid behind the sofa. What part of "I want to be alone" did I not understand?

I was overwrought about my cat dying. I knew this would be the scariest loss I'd experienced since I gave up drinking. I worried about the incoming grief: when I would lose him, how it might rearrange my heart. But here's the problem with worry— it doesn't actually *do* anything.

A cancerous mass was growing on the side of his face. He looked like a squirrel hiding nuts in one cheek. I measured the growth with my fingers each morning. From a nut to a lime to a baseball. I would meet his eyes before we went to sleep. *You have to tell me when it's time,* I would say, knowing full well he could not.

One afternoon, I kissed his nose, and only half of his little face squinted. *That's odd.* I ran one hand over his eyes, and his left eye refused to close. It had turned glassy. I called Jennifer at her vet clinic, and her soft voice told me what I already knew. The next morning, she came to my house in her blue scrubs and sat cross-legged on the floor of my bedroom and let me hold Bubba as she inserted the IV into his tiny orange paw.

"This will be fast," she said. "Are you ready?" And I was not, but I was as ready as I was going to be.

She pushed the plunger on the first syringe, and he made a purr like an engine coming to a stop. His body slumped in my arms. I don't remember the second syringe. What I remember is opening my eyes, and Jennifer leaning over him with a stethoscope, and the way she met my gaze to tell me he was gone. His body was warm against my face.

My mind couldn't keep pace with the change. I carried Bubba to Jennifer's car and lay him gingerly in the front passenger seat. As I walked back into my carriage house, tears dripping off my chin, what I expected to find, more than anything, was him at the top of the stairs to help me through this ordeal.

The pain of his loss was enormous, but I never once thought: *Drinking would make this better. You know what this horrible day calls for? Booze.* I finally understood alcohol was not a cure for pain; it was merely a postponement.

I don't know when it happened, but I stopped longing for the drink. I'm not saying I never miss drinking, because I do on occasion, but the craving and the clawing is gone. Happy hour comes and goes, and I don't notice. A foamy pint no longer beckons to me like a crooked finger. Bar signs lit up with blinking neon look exactly like what they are: beautiful distractions.

This shift seemed impossible at one time. The woman hiding in the closet knew her life was over, and she was on some artificial lung now. I wish I could have known how much easier it would be on this side.

For so many years, I was stuck in a spin cycle of worry and questioning. *Am I an alcoholic? Is alcoholism a "disease"? What if this, or that, or the other thing?* Overthinkers are the most exhausting alcoholics. I have left a trail of soggy Kleenex that could stretch to the sun, but the equation is simple. When I cut out alcohol, my life got better. When I cut out alcohol, my spirit came back. An evolved life requires balance. Sometimes you have to cut out one thing to find balance everywhere else.

I watch women at bars sometimes. I watch them holding the wineglass in their hands, the wet curve of the lip forever finding the light. I watch them in their skirts small as cocktail napkins and their skyscraper heels, but I don't envy them anymore. Maybe at some advanced age, we get the gift of being happy where we are. Or maybe where I am right now got a whole lot easier to take.

A woman I know told me a story once, about how she'd always been the girl in the front row at live shows. Pushing her way to the place where the spotlight burned tracers in her eyes and the speakers rattled her insides. When she quit drinking, she missed that full-throttle part of herself, but then she realized: *Sobriety is full throttle.* No earplugs. No safe distance. Everything at its highest volume. All the complications of the world, vibrating your sternum.

I go to meetings, and I can't believe the grief people walk through. Losing their children, losing their spouse. I can't believe how sheltered I've been. Here I am, undone by the loss of my 17-year-old cat.

"I wish I was tougher," I complained to my friend Mary.

"Well, you're not tough," she told me, and I laughed. "Tough is a posture anyway. You're something better. You're resilient."

I still cry most mornings when I awake and he's not there. I hate looking up in the second-story window where he will never sit, breaking into excited noise when I come through the gate. But I know how to start over now, which means I can start over as many times as I need. I'm all too aware that the biggest challenges of my life are still in front of me. And I feel a little worried about that. Mostly, I feel prepared.

It's funny how I used to think drinking made me a grown-up. Back when I was a little girl, I would slip a crystal wineglass off the shelf of my parents' cabinet, and the heft of it felt like independence. I played cocktail party, not tea party, because that's what glamorous adults on TV did. But drinking was actually an extended adolescence for me. An insanely fun, wonderfully complicated, emotionally arrested adolescence. And quitting drinking was the first true act of my adulthood. A coming-of-age for a woman who came of age a long time ago.

⁓

EACH YEAR, I drive out to see Anna. It takes ten hours to get to her West Texas home from Dallas, but I don't mind. The rumble of the tires is like a meditative hum. The perpetual motion shuts down my brain. The sky is a blue that contains many blues: the milky blue of the prairie, the electric blue of the desert.

I listen to pop songs in the car, three-minute blasts of

feel-good, a buzz that never fails. My Honda is like a portable '70s disco: ELO, the BeeGees, Queen. As I drive across the empty roads, I sing with the surrender that booze used to bring, and I wonder if it would ever be possible to take this starlit feeling and somehow stretch it across the rest of my life.

Anna and I have had 20 years of these reunions. Twenty years of hugs and how-was-the-drives, and both of us politely disagreeing over who is going to carry the bags to the doorstep. And whenever Anna and I feel far apart, even as we are sitting next to each other on the couch, I tell myself 20 years was a good run.

The distance of these past years has spooked me. A couple years ago, I came out to visit, and we had a tense disagreement in her car. It was nighttime, and we were stopped at the railroad that cuts through town, the red light flashing as the boxcars hurtled past. I said to her, with too much grit in my voice, "I don't think you know how hard it is to be single and alone."

And she said, with perfect calm, "I don't think you know how hard it is to be married with a kid."

It was the full summary of the standoff we'd been having for years. The white arm of the gate lifted, and we crossed the tracks.

This time, I want it to be different. I know that her life has changed, but I want to believe that I might still have a place in it. I turn into the gravel road that leads to her place. I pull up to find Anna doing her jokey dance, guiding me into the driveway. Alice stands behind the screen door, watching. It's hard to imagine a world farther from New York. There's a clothesline on her patio, an ocotillo cactus growing in her front yard.

"You made it," she says, and I smile. "I did."

The next afternoon, we drive through the red-rock mountains heading to a natural spring. The vista makes you wonder why anyone ever moved to a city. I keep feeling the urge for some monumental conversation, but Anna and I have had two decades of monumental conversations. Maybe what we need are smaller conversations now. So we talk about the latest *New Yorker*. We talk about films. We talk about the view outside the window, a view we share for a change.

Best friends. For so long, those two words contained music to me, but also a threat of possession. I hung the words like pelts in my room. I had best friends for every life phase, every season. The words were meant to express love, but wasn't I also expressing competition? There was a ranking, and I needed to be at the top. Anna's closest friend now is a woman she works with at the legal aid office. They take care of each other's children and giggle with the familiarity of twins. It's exactly the kind of companionship Anna and I had once, and it stings sometimes when I feel replaced, but I wouldn't wish anything different for her.

I know Anna and I will never be friends like we were at 19, because we'll never be 19 again. I also know this is nothing I did. That while drinking wrecks precious things, it never wrecked our friendship. Sometimes people drift in and out of your life, and the real agony is fighting it. You can gulp down an awful lot of seawater, trying to change the tides.

At the springs, Anna and I lay down a blanket on the grass and splay out our imperfect bodies. I tell her about what I'm writing, and she talks about Alice's new Montessori preschool. We don't share the same language anymore, but we are both trying to learn the other's vocabulary.

I wonder if our lives will track closer after I have a baby, and she once again becomes the mentor she was to me in my younger days. Then again, I may never have a baby, and I feel all right with that. So many women my age are torn up over the question mark of motherhood, but on this topic—if nothing else—I feel a total zen. I don't know what comes next. It's like a novel whose ending I haven't read yet.

The sun is hot, and pools of sweat start dripping down our bare bellies. We walk out to the spring and touch a toe in the water. It's bracingly cold. A short diving board leads out into the middle of the murky pool, and we stand there like kids, hunched and laughing, our skin covered with goose bumps.

"You go," I say, nudging her, and she says, "No, you go." And we giggle until she gathers herself up, serious now. "OK, do you want me to go?" And I nod. So she walks out on the platform, like she always has, and jumps first.

❦

ONE SUNDAY MORNING, my mother and I are having coffee. We're still in our yoga clothes, sitting on the empty patio of a café. Out of nowhere, she says, "I'm just so glad you're sober."

My mom didn't say much about my drinking for a long time, and now that the subject is out in the open, I feel uncomfortable dwelling here. The words can make me feel stuck, branded. I'm four years sober now. When do these pronouncements end?

But I understand my mother needs to give voice to these feelings. She is an emotional blurter. In the middle of family dinner, she'll say to me and my brother, "I just love you two kids so much," and it's like: OK, but can you pass the chicken?

My mother stares at her teacup, getting a contemplative look in her eye. "I wish I could have been there more for you when you were a little girl," she says, and her green eyes turn watery.

"Mom, stop," I say, waving off the emotional charge of the conversation. "Don't you like who I am?"

She nods that yes, she does.

"Do you think you screwed up so badly that it requires all this apologizing?"

She shakes her head that no, she doesn't. She tries to explain gently, what I might not understand: the impossible hope of parenthood, the need to shelter your child from pain. It's hard to live with the mistakes, she says. She wishes she'd been better.

I do understand. We all live in the long shadow of the person we could have been. I regret how selfish and irresponsible I've been as their daughter. How many things I took for granted. My mother's constant emotional nourishment. My father's hard work and unwavering support.

I have lunch each month with my dad now. He is different than the man who raised me. Looser, funnier, and more engaged, faster with his smile. He still reads the newspaper every day. Watches the evening news. There is so much more kicking around in his head than I ever gave him credit for. Just because someone is quiet doesn't mean they have nothing to say.

One afternoon, we start talking about drinking. My dad quit ten years ago, worrying the alcohol would interfere with his medications. Though he'd never been much of a drinker when I was a little girl, by the time I was in college, his consumption had crept into the armchair-drinker red zone. He could put away a bottle a night without realizing it.

Because he quit so easily, and without complaint, I assumed it wasn't a big sacrifice. But he tells me that's not true. It had been rough. He still misses it all the time. "I would definitely say I have alcoholic tendencies," he tells me, and I look at him. Once again: *Who* are *you?*

In the four years of my sobriety, he has never said these words to me. *Alcoholic tendencies.* I continue to be startled by how much of my personality derives from him. My self-consciousness, my humor, my anxiety. I may look and talk like my mother, but I am equal parts (if not more) this man. What else has my dad not told me? How much more has he kept inside, because no one ever thought to ask? And do I have enough time to dig it out?

I'm aware of the ticking clock. My mother loses her keys too often, and she forgets what she's saying in midsentence. My dad loses his balance when he stands in one place too long. Neurological problems in his feet. One evening, his legs give out while we're standing in a line, and he slumps to the ground right next to me, as though he's been shot. I can't help noticing the effects of aging are an awful lot like the effects of drinking. Loss of balance. Loss of consciousness. Loss of memory.

We spend all these years drinking away our faculties and then all these years trying to hold on to them. When my friends share stories about their parents fighting Alzheimer's, I hear echoes of my own behavior. *He keeps taking off all his clothes. She won't stop cussing. He disappears in a fog.*

A life is bookended by forgetting, as though memory forms the tunnel that leads into and out of a human body. I'm friends with a married couple who have a two-year-old. She is all grunt and grab, a pint-size party animal in a polka-dot romper, and we laugh at how much she reminds us of our drunken selves. She shoves her hands in her diaper and demands a cookie. She dips one finger in queso and rubs it on her lips. Any hint of music becomes a need to dance. Oh, that child loves to dance. Spinning in a circle. Slapping her big toddler belly. One eye squinted, her tongue poking out of her mouth, as though this movement balances her somehow.

I recognize this as the freedom drinking helped me to recapture. A magnificent place where no one's judgment mattered, my needs were met, and my emotions could explode in a tantrum.

And when I was finally spent, someone would scoop me up in their arms and place me safely in my crib again.

I wonder sometimes if anything could have prevented me from becoming an alcoholic, or if drinking was simply my fate. It's a question my friends with kids ask me, too, because they worry. How can they know if their kids are drinking too much? What should they do? I feel such sympathy for parents, plugging their fingers in the leaky dam of the huge and troubling world. But I'm not sure my parents could have done anything to keep me away from the bottomless pitcher of early adulthood. I was probably going to find my way to that bar stool no matter what. Addiction is a function of two factors: genetics and culture. On both counts, the cards were stacked against me. Still, I know, I was the one who played the hand.

There is no single formula that makes a problem drinker. I've heard many competing stories. Parents who were too strict, parents who were too lax. A kid who got too much attention, and a kid who didn't get enough. The reason I drank is because I became certain booze could save me. And I clung to this delusion for 25 years.

I think each generation reinvents rebellion. My generation drank. But the future of addiction is pills. Good-bye, liquor cabinet, hello, medicine cabinet. A kid who pops Oxycontin at 15 doesn't really get the big deal about taking heroin at 19. They're basically the same thing. Growing up, I thought substance abuse fell into two camps: drinking, which was fine, and everything else, which was not. Now I understand that all substance abuse lies on the same continuum.

But I'm not sad or embarrassed to be an alcoholic anymore. I get irritated when I hear parents use that jokey shorthand: God, I hope my kid doesn't end up in rehab. Or: God, I hope my kid

doesn't end up in therapy. I understand the underlying wish—
I hope my kid grows up happy and safe. When we say things
like that, though, we underscore the false belief that people who
seek help are failures and people who don't seek help are a success. It's not true. Some of the healthiest, most accomplished
people I know went to both rehab and therapy, and I've known
some sick motherfuckers who managed to avoid both.

When I sit in rooms with people once considered washed up,
I feel at home. I've come to think of being an alcoholic as one
of the best things that ever happened to me. Those low years
startled me awake. I stopped despairing for what I didn't get and
I began cherishing what I did.

⌒

IN NOVEMBER OF 2013, I flew back to Paris. It had been seven
years since I staggered into that gutter on the wrong side of 2 am,
and I had left the city saying I'd never return. Classic drunk
logic: Paris was the problem, not me. This is what drinkers do.
We close doors. Avoid that guy. Never go back to that restaurant. Seek out clean ledgers. We get pushed around by history
because we refuse to live with it.

I wanted to go back. I wanted to find out what I could. There
were only two people on the planet who could help me back-
fill the events of that night, and Johnson's was the only name I
knew.

Entering the hotel again was like walking into a snapshot in
the pages of an old photo album. There was the gleaming white
stone of the floor. There was the plate glass window. And there
was the ghostly feeling: *This is the place.*

"I stayed here once, years ago," I told the guy behind the counter. He was young, accommodating, and spoke perfect English.

I asked him, "You wouldn't be able to tell me the number of the room I stayed in, would you?"

"I'm so sorry," he said. The hotel had changed ownership. Its records didn't date back that far.

I expected as much. My story took place a mere seven years ago, but tracking down details of the Paris trip felt like trying to find the wedding jars from Cana. My old emails had been purged by Hotmail. My assigning editors had no record of where I'd stayed and no memory of the hotel's name. I couldn't find my credit card statements, having closed those cards years ago. I tried the bookkeeper at the magazine, who said she might be able to break into old records and find my receipts, but it required a password from someone on vacation. In this technology age, we talk about information living forever—as though an infallible archive is the burden we must bear—but we never talk about how much information gets lost. Whole chunks of our history can disappear in the blip of an HTML code.

"There was a guy who worked at the concierge desk named Johnson," I said to the young man. "Does he work here anymore?"

Johnson, Johnson. He checked with a few coworkers. "Nobody here knows that name, no."

I figured he was long gone, but I had to ask. I was afraid to see him again, but I also wanted to hear his side of the story. How I sounded to him. What he saw in my face. He called me once. I was at a fancy Thanksgiving dinner party at Stephanie's, a few days after I got home, and to hear his voice on the other end of the line was like a hand grabbing me around the throat. I couldn't figure out how he got my number. *What the fuck, dude? What the fuck?* After I calmed down, I remembered. I gave it to him.

"Can you think of anyone else at the hotel who might know this Johnson guy?" I asked the young clerk behind the counter.

The kid crunched his brow. "The concierge who works in the morning," he said. "He's been here for 25 years. If anyone knows this man, he will."

I thanked him, and spent the rest of the day retracing the steps I took all those years ago, a guided tour of my own troubled past. I was relieved by how many of my memories were correct. Some details I had wrong. The sheets were scratchier than I remembered. The hotel door a revolving entryway, not an automated push.

As I walked to the Eiffel Tower, I tested my own recall. There will be a crêpe stand two blocks from here, I told myself. There will be a road that spirals out into paved streets. And I got excited by how good I was at this game, just like I was good at the childhood board game of Memory, where twinned pictures hide on the other side of square cards. Yes, the whole scene was exactly as I remembered it. The crunch of gravel under my boots. The November wind slicing through my coat. The flickering of the Eiffel Tower on the hour, thousands of lightbulbs going off at once. The gasp of the crowd. The kisses, the children lifted onto shoulders. It happened then, and it's happening now. It happens many times, every day, and so I don't quite understand why it gave me such a thrill to think: *I was here once. I remember this.*

I remember this. Why is a tug into the past so satisfying? Wise men tell us to live in the present. Be here now. Stand toe-to-toe with each moment as it arrives. And yet, I love to be pulled into the corridors of my past. That home where I once lived. That street I used to walk alone. Writers build monuments to our former selves, our former lives, because we're always hoping to return to the past and master it somehow, find the missing puzzle piece that helps everything make sense.

I woke early the next morning to speak to Guillaume, the

concierge of long standing. "There was a guy who used to work the night shift," I said.

Guillaume listened as I explained in broad strokes, leaving out nearly all details. He shoved his glasses up the bridge of his nose a few times. "Night guys, we don't know them much," he said. "People come in and out of here all the time."

"Of course," I said. "Thanks so much," and I left before he could see that I was starting to cry.

Why was I crying? Why did I feel foolish at that moment? Maybe because I knew the unedited story of how that man came into my life, and I hurt for what brought about our intersection. Perhaps the trip felt futile. I had come all this way to track down someone who could not be found. Or perhaps there was tender sense memory in the spot where I was standing. I could remember standing at the same desk seven years before. How leveled I was.

I left the hotel, and climbed into a taxi that took me to an airport that carried me across an ocean and all the way home. I did not have the answers, but I had the satisfaction of having looked, which is sometimes the thing you need to move on.

∾

IT'S ABOUT 15 minutes till 8 pm, and I'm sitting on a bench near the location of a dime store where I used to steal lipstick when I was 12. I would slip the glossy black tubes in my pocket, because I had discovered I could, and because I wanted more than what I had been given. The dime store is long gone, replaced by a gourmet burger bar, where the only stealing being done is by the owners: $12 for a burger with truffle aioli.

Across the street is an unmarked door leading into a room where people who are not drinking gather and try to be better.

I'm meeting a younger woman who reached out to me one night, over email, after finding a few of my stories online.

"I'm sorry you have to meet me like this," she says. She apologizes for a lot of things. How frazzled she is. How sad and confused. She apologizes when she cries, and she apologizes that I have to spend time with her, and I point out I am *choosing* to spend time with her.

She doesn't believe me, and I don't blame her. I never believed it when people said stuff like that to me. *Yeah, whatever*, I would think. *Why would you want to spend time with a mess like me?*

AA reminds you how much of our stories are the same. This is also what literature, and science, and religion will remind you as well. We all want to believe our pain is singular—that no one else has felt this way—but our pain is ordinary, which is both a blessing and a curse. It means we're not unique. But it also means we're not alone. One of the best sayings I ever heard someone toss out at a meeting: If you've fucked a zebra, someone else has fucked two. I haven't seen it hung next to the other slogans yet, but I'm hoping.

The woman draws her purse onto her lap. Her life feels clouded, she says. She's not sure who she is, or what she wants anymore. She tells me her story, which is carved with her own particulars, but the template is familiar. We arrive at a place of reckoning as strangers to ourselves. When she starts to cry, she reaches for Kleenex in her purse, apologizing once more.

"You should have seen how much I cried when I quit," I said. "Insane tears."

"It's hard for me to believe you were ever like this," she says.

I try to explain to her. The despair, the frailty, the emotional hurly-burly—I lived there once, too. And she stares at me like I'm trying to sell her something.

"It's just that I look at you, and it's clear you know who you are," she says. I am wearing sweatpants pulled from the floor, because I was running late, and no makeup. Not my most Hollywood look. But it's also true that I am not befogged with need and wanting anymore.

I don't know how it happened, or exactly how long it took. But I looked up one day and discovered, to my own shock as much as anyone else's, that I was something approaching the woman I might like to be.

"I was in the exact same place as you are," I say, tears filling up my eyes. "I was lost for a very long time." And even if she doesn't understand, I can see that she believes me.

As for whether she'll stop drinking or not, I can't tell you. I have no idea. Every sobriety tale is a cliffhanger. None of us knows how our story ends.

But these conversations are good for me. They deliver me from my own sorrow. They remind me of my usefulness. They keep me from forgetting. How I got here, how I climbed out. I forgot too many things for far too long. Not just what we did last night, but who I was, where I wanted to go. I don't do that anymore. Now I remember.

ABOUT THE AUTHOR

SARAH HEPOLA'S writing has appeared in the *New York Times Magazine*, *The New Republic*, *Glamour*, *The Guardian*, *The Morning News*, and *Salon*, where she is an editor. She has worked as a music critic, travel writer, film reviewer, sex blogger, beauty columnist, and a high school English teacher. Her website is sarahhepola.com. She lives in Dallas.

TWO ROADS

Stories . . . voices . . . places . . . lives

We hope you enjoyed *Blackout*. If you'd like to know more about this book or any other title on our list, please go to www.tworoadsbooks.com

For news on forthcoming Two Roads titles, please sign up for our newsletter.

enquiries@tworoadsbooks.com

TwoRoadsBooks